NEW
Low Fat Recipes

NEW
Low Fat Recipes

by Anny Mauder

with a foreword by
Sir Francis Avery Jones CBE, FRCP

**Nutritional Therapy for
Heart disease, Weight control,
Digestive, Gall bladder and
Pancreas disorders**

W. FOULSHAM & CO. LTD
LONDON · NEW YORK · TORONTO
CAPE TOWN · SYDNEY

*To my husband, whose need caused
the book to be written and whose
help brought it to completion.*

W. Foulsham & Company Limited
Yeovil Road, Slough, Berkshire, SL1 4JH

ISBN 0-572-01335-3

Recipes first published in *Fat Free... that's me.*

Printed in Great Britain by St. Edmundsbury Press,
Bury St. Edmunds, Suffolk.

CONTENTS

WHY FAT-FREE COOKING?

As a physician who has spent a lifetime treating patients with digestive disorders, I know that there are many people who will be helped by this book. Medically there are two main groups of individuals who will find it particularly helpful. First, there is a group of people who are perfectly healthy in every other way but who, all their lives, have had a bilious tendency, easily upset by rich, fatty foods. As children, they were thought to be difficult; as adults, pernickety. However, the fault is not in their minds but in their body chemistry. Lacking certain enzymes, they are unable to complete the digestion of certain foods, particularly fatty foods, and these products of incomplete digestion circulate in the blood giving rise to nausea, biliousness, headaches and general misery. Often it is a condition which runs in the family.

Second, there are patients who have already developed a physical disease causing partial or complete failure of the gall bladder. The mechanism of this organ is usually beautifully coordinated and, when fatty food is eaten, the gall bladder very quickly begins to contract, spurting bile into the upper intestine where it emulsifies the fat as it leaves the stomach. If the flow of bile is reduced, the capacity for digesting fat without discomfort is correspondingly less. Sometimes there are physical diseases affecting another of the digestive organs -- the pancreas or the small intestine itself -- and only small amounts of fat in the diet can be tolerated. Such people know from experience that more than a certain amount of fat will cause appreciable discomfort and they, too, will welcome this book.

It has become increasingly appreciated on both sides of the Atlantic that our present-day diet contains too much fat, particularly animal fat, and general encouragement is being given to reduce fat intake. Certainly those with a family history of heart disease are particularly advised to do so. For such people this book gives invaluable guidance for tasty low fat meals.

Sir Francis Avery Jones, CBE, FRCP
Consulting Physician – Central Middlesex Hospital
Consulting Gastroenterologist – St Mark's Hospital and the
Consultant Emeritus in Gastroenterology to the Royal Navy

INTRODUCTION

New Low Fat Recipes is a completely new approach to one of mankind's main enjoyments in life – good food, but with a low fat content. You will be surprised at the number of attractive and varied dishes you can make without ever having butter or any other fat in your kitchen. You will find, too, that your kitchen is as clean after cooking as it was before. There is no fat splashing and nothing gets sticky, thus saving a lot of time and effort.

One day the problem and necessity of eating fatless meals came into my life, and I realized that I could not buy any ready-made foods to help the daily menu. As I keep open house for lots of friends and visitors, the challenge was to make my meals as interesting and varied as if I had not been restricted in any way.

I soon realized that there was virtually no literature about fat-free cooking, and I had to invent and adapt as well as I could. When I declared that everyone who ate with me would have to eat the same diet, I got some very sceptical looks. But by and by more and more people asked me for the different recipes, until I realized that not only did my cooking please many people but also, and more important, there was a great demand for such recipes. The results of this cooking are exciting and delicious, as well as unusual, but it is essential to adhere to the given ingredients.

A fat-free diet is a misnomer, since there is no totally fat-free food; however, the diet described in this book aims at recipes containing not more than about 7 to 10 per cent of fat, compared with, say, a piece of cheese which contains at least 30 per cent. Never before have there been so many overweight people who need a low fat diet. There are many who have a very low fat tolerance in their digestive system, or who suffer from conditions such as heart disease, when a low fat diet is essential.

I hope that my experience and success in keeping myself, my family and our friends healthy and slim will help many others who find themselves in need of similar help.

Please do read the instructions which follow as they give a few guidelines which are essential to observe.

SOME TIPS TO REMEMBER

All recipes are for four people, unless stated otherwise.

For each recipe cooking and preparation times (total time) are given.

In many of the recipes I use a pressure cooker in preference to an ordinary saucepan, as it saves two-thirds of the cooking time, keeps the juices in and does not steam up the kitchen. 'H' pressure means high pressure. For those who do not like pressure cookers, a normal saucepan and lid will do. Cooking time has to be adjusted.

Never cook meat and vegetables together as the fat from the meat soaks into the vegetables.

Use skimmed milk in preference to normal milk; but if you do use normal milk, thin it slightly or remove the top cream.

Use low fat yoghurt or make your own from skimmed milk.

Use only low fat cheese.

The commercially sold low fat curd cheese and low fat soft cheese has 8 to 10 per cent fat content and may not be suitable for some users of this book.

Cottage cheese is always low fat (under 1 per cent), but has a somewhat rough texture.

There is a 'skimmed milk soft cheese' obtainable in some supermarkets and food shops which has a smooth texture and a fat content of under 1 per cent and is suitable for all the recipes.

When using green and red peppers always remove the pith as well as the seeds.

Ask your butcher to cut off all fat, but additionally always trim the meat yourself.

Beef is permissible, but the cheaper cuts are better; steak is marbled with fat which you do not see. I have found the eye of the blade the leanest joint and most butchers will cut it out for you; it can be roasted as well as boiled or stewed.

Allow all meat juice to stand and cool until a hard crust of fat forms, which you can easily remove. Only then can you use it for gravy or sauce.

Unless I have plenty of time, I freeze de-fatted meat juice and use it as stock for a sauce or gravy when I need it to accompany a joint or meat course. (You can freeze it in small containers in the freezing compartment of your refrigerator if you have no deep freeze.)

Whenever you can, cook meat on a trivet – it allows it to cook without swimming in its own fat.

Skin fish where possible, as the skin contains fat. Poultry skin also contains fat, but as you cannot roast it without skin, remove the skin after cooking, and do not eat it.

If you add a spoonful of yoghurt to sauces or soups, you get the consistency of cream and, if anything, a slightly finer taste.

In cakes I use up to two egg yolks; as the amount of fat in the yolk spreads throughout the whole cake, the total fat intake in one or two slices remains very little. Cakes can be made with egg white only, if preferred.

Always use non-stick frying pans and non-stick cake or bread tins as the fatless foods stick to normal tins.

It is vital never to use tinned food or ready-made preparations without checking on the fat content.

Recipes with asterisks* are high in cholesterol though low in fat content.

FORBIDDEN FOODS

All fried foods
Bacon
Fatty meat, eg, pork, goose, lamb
Oily fish, eg, sardines, herrings, salmon,
    mackerel
Cheese, except low fat varieties
Cream, mock cream, ice cream
Butter, fat or oil
Margarine
Cream crackers
Mayonnaise
Nuts, except chestnuts
Peanut butter
Chocolates, toffee
Cocoa and similar beverages
Olives
Avocado pears
Shortbread, biscuits

ESSENTIAL TOOLS

Non-stick frying pan
Blender
Non-stick cake tin *or* loose bottomed cake tin
Non-stick bread tin
Grater
Whisk and bowl

OPTIONAL TOOLS

Fondue set
Pressure cooker

STOCKS & SAUCES

CHICKEN STOCK

	Metric	Imperial	American
Bones and skin of boiled or roasted chicken	1	1	1
Salt			
Bouquet garni			

Put the chicken bones and skin into a pressure cooker. Season with a little salt, add bouquet garni, cover with water and cook at H pressure for 30 minutes.

Strain off the liquid into a container and leave to cool. When cold remove all the fat from the top, cover the container and keep in the refrigerator or freeze and store in the freezer.

Note: Chicken stock will keep for only a day or two, in the ordinary compartments of a refrigerator, unless it is re-boiled daily. But the liquid can be frozen and kept for as long as your freezer allows.

Total time: 40 mins.

MEAT STOCK

This is a liquid base for soups and sauces. It can be refrigerated for a few days in a covered container, or frozen for as long as your freezer allows.

	Metric	Imperial	American
Lean beef, chopped	450 g	1 lb	1 lb
Beef or veal bones	900 g	2 lb	2 lb
Carrots, peeled and chopped	2	2	2
Medium size onions, peeled and chopped	2	2	2
Stick of celery, washed and chopped	1	1	1
Bouquet garni or freshly chopped parsley, thyme, marjoram and sage			
Salt and pepper			

Put all the ingredients into a pressure cooker and season with salt and pepper. Cover with water and cook under H pressure for 30 minutes, then strain off the liquid into a container and leave to cool.

When cold, remove all the fat, then cover the container and keep in the refrigerator, or freeze the liquid and store in the freezer.

Note: The boiled meat can be used as it is or with a sauce in a casserole.

Total time: 40 mins.

BROWN GRAVY

	Metric	Imperial	American
Cornflour	2 tsp	2 tsp	2 tsp
Water or meat stock			
(Page 14)	600 ml	1 pt	2½ cups
Marmite or Oxo	½ tbsp	½ tbsp	½ tbsp
Salt and pepper			
Red wine (optional)			

Blend cornflour in a little of the liquid until smooth. Heat slowly in saucepan, stirring all the time. Add Marmite or Oxo (if you have used water) and blend. Add remainder of liquid and salt and pepper to taste. Red wine can be used to replace up to half the stock or water. Bring to the boil and simmer gently for a few minutes. Serve hot in a sauceboat.

Notes: This goes well with most meats. If you have meat stock you do not need Marmite or Oxo.

Total time: 15 mins.

BASIC WHITE SAUCE

	Metric	Imperial	American
Flour (plain or self-raising)	2 tbsp	2 tbsp	2 tbsp
Milk or yoghurt	150 ml	¼ pt	⅔ cup
Water or chicken stock	375 ml	¾ pt	2 cups
Salt			
White wine (optional)			

Blend the flour in a little of the milk, until smooth. Heat slowly, gradually adding the rest of the milk and water or stock. Stir continuously until it reaches the consistency of thick cream. Add salt to taste. Simmer gently for several minutes to remove the floury taste. (White wine can replace up to half the water or stock.)

Note: From this base a large variety of excellent sauces can be prepared to suit many dishes.

Total time: 10 mins.

BASIC BROWN SAUCE

	Metric	Imperial	American
Milk or yoghurt	150 ml	¼ pt	⅔ cup
Flour	2 tbsp	2 tbsp	2 tbsp
Meat stock	375 ml	¾ pt	2 cups
Gravy browning	3 drops	3 drops	3 drops
Salt and pepper			

Mix milk and flour to a smooth paste. Add meat stock, gravy browning and salt to taste. Simmer over a low flame, stirring all the time, until it thickens to the desired consistency.

Note: This is used as a base for some of the sauces which follow, and for stew.

Total time: 15 mins.

HORSERADISH SAUCE

	Metric	Imperial	American
Basic white sauce (Page 16)	600 ml	1 pt	2½ cups
Horseradish, grated	2 tbsp	2 tbsp	2 tbsp
Yoghurt	1 tbsp	1 tbsp	1 tbsp

Make the basic white sauce and stir horseradish into it. Reheat and, just before serving, add the yoghurt. Serve hot with beef.

Total time: 10 mins.

MUSHROOM SAUCE

	Metric	Imperial	American
Basic brown sauce (Page 17)	600 ml	1 pt	2½ cups
Mushrooms, washed and sliced	100 g	4 oz	¼ lb
Salt and pepper			

Make the basic brown sauce. Barely cover the bottom of a saucepan with water. Add the mushrooms and salt and pepper to taste. Simmer for a few minutes until tender. Add to the basic sauce, stirring well.

Serve hot, with meat, mince loaf or stew.

Total time: 10 mins.

TOMATO SAUCE

	Metric	Imperial	American
Basic white sauce (Page 16)	600 ml	1 pt	2½ cups
Can of tomato purée	150 g	5 oz	5 oz
Small onion, peeled and grated	½	½	½
Sugar	½ tbsp	½ tbsp	½ tbsp
Vinegar	½ tbsp	½ tbsp	½ tbsp
Salt			
Basil (optional)	1 pinch	1 pinch	1 pinch

Make the basic white sauce. Add the tomato purée, onion, sugar, vinegar, salt and basil. Heat and simmer for a few minutes, stirring well.

Serve hot with pasta, fish, rice dishes and meat loaf.

Total time: 15 mins.

CHEESE SAUCE

	Metric	Imperial	American
Basic white sauce (Page 16)	600 ml	1 pt	2½ cups
Curd or cottage cheese	225 g	8 oz	½ lb

Make the basic white sauce. Add the cheese and mix well. Heat and simmer, stirring all the time, until smooth.

Serve hot with lasagne, cauliflower, leeks, fish or pasta.

Curd cheese gives a much better consistency and appearance than cottage cheese.

Total time: 10 mins.

PARSLEY SAUCE

	Metric	Imperial	American
Basic white sauce (Page 16)	600 ml	1 pt	2½ cups
Freshly chopped parsley	½ tbsp	½ tbsp	½ tbsp
Juice of lemon	½	½	½

Make the basic white sauce. Add the parsley and lemon juice and stir well. Serve hot with fish, cauliflower, celery and other vegetables.

Total time: 10 mins.

SAUCE PIQUANTE

	Metric	Imperial	American
Basic white sauce (Page 16)	600 ml	1 pt	2½ cups
Freshly chopped parsley or chives	1 tsp	1 tsp	1 tsp
French mustard	½ tsp	½ tsp	½ tsp
Capers, chopped	½ tbsp	½ tbsp	½ tbsp
Juice of lemon	½	½	½

Make the basic white sauce. Add the parsley or chives, French mustard, capers and lemon juice. Stir well and heat. Serve hot, either in a sauceboat or poured directly over fish.

For variety add 3 drops of Worcestershire sauce and 1 tablespoon of tomato ketchup to the sauce.

Total time: 10 mins.

BARBECUE SAUCE

	Metric	Imperial	American
Medium size onion, peeled	1	1	1
Mushrooms, washed	175 g	6 oz	6 oz
Green pepper, de-seeded	1	1	1
Clove garlic, peeled	1	1	1
Tomato purée	3 tbsp	3 tbsp	3 tbsp
Water	300 ml	½ pt	1¼ cups
Salt			
Bay leaf	1	1	1

Put the onion, mushrooms, green pepper, garlic and tomato purée into a blender. Add water and season with a little salt. Liquidize. Pour the mixture into a saucepan, add the bay leaf and simmer for about 20 minutes. Remove the bay leaf and serve hot or cold.

Total time: 10 mins.

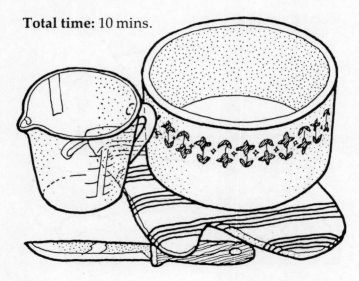

CUMBERLAND SAUCE

	Metric	Imperial	American
Juice and finely grated rind of oranges	2	2	2
Salt and pepper			
French mustard	1 tbsp	1 tbsp	1 tbsp
Worcestershire sauce	3 drops	3 drops	3 drops
Redcurrant jelly	250 g	8 oz	½ lb

Put the orange juice and rind, salt and pepper, French mustard, Worcestershire sauce and redcurrant jelly into a saucepan. Stir and simmer until the jelly dissolves. Put into sauceboat or jug and allow to cool.

Note: This is a special sauce for all cold meats.

Total time: 15 mins.

SWEET AND SOUR SAUCE

	Metric	Imperial	American
Cornflour	1½ tbsp	1½ tbsp	1½ tbsp
Pineapple juice	600 ml	1 pt	2½ cups
Vinegar	1 tbsp	1 tbsp	1 tbsp
Brown sugar	2 tbsp	2 tbsp	2 tbsp
Tomato ketchup	2 tbsp	2 tbsp	2 tbsp

Blend cornflour with a little of the pineapple juice until smooth. Heat slowly in saucepan, then add the rest of the pineapple juice and the vinegar, brown sugar and tomato ketchup. Simmer, stirring continually, until the sauce thickens and glazes.

Serve hot with chicken risotto or cold with cold meats.

Total time: 15 mins.

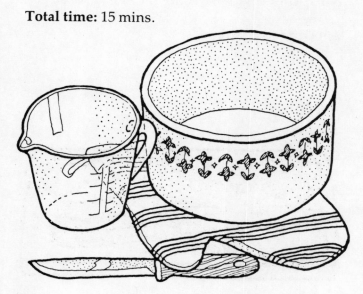

PAPRIKA SAUCE

	Metric	Imperial	American
Basic white sauce (Page 16)	600 ml	1 pt	2½ cups
Sweet paprika	2 tsp	2 tsp	2 tsp
Tomato purée	½ tbsp	½ tbsp	½ tbsp
Yoghurt	½ tbsp	½ tbsp	½ tbsp

Make the basic white sauce. Add the paprika and tomato purée. Heat slowly and simmer for a few minutes. Just before serving add the yoghurt.

Excellent with stewed beef, veal, chicken and meat loaf.

Total time: 10 mins.

BREAKFAST CEREAL

BREAKFAST CEREAL

Equal amounts of:
Rolled oats
Sultanas
Grape nuts
Bran
Brown sugar

Mix all the ingredients together and keep in an airtight plastic container. To serve, scoop out three tablespoons per person into individual cereal bowls, add a little milk and leave to stand while you prepare tea or coffee.

Note: From time to time, prepare this breakfast cereal in large amounts so there is always some ready for use.

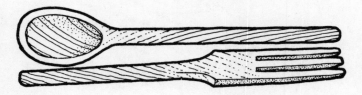

SOUPS

ASPARAGUS SOUP

	Metric	Imperial	American
Basic white sauce			
(Page 16)	750 ml	1½ pt	3 cups
Canned asparagus	225 g	8 oz	½ lb
White wine (optional)	150 ml	¼ pt	⅔ cup
Salt			
Yoghurt			

Prepare the basic white sauce.

Cut the asparagus into short pieces and add, with the liquid from the can, to the white sauce. Add white wine, season to taste and bring to the boil. Pour into individual soup bowls. Add a dessertspoon of yoghurt to each bowl and serve hot with thin slices of toast.

Total time: 15 mins.

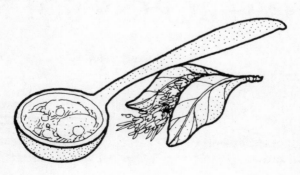

ARTICHOKE SOUP

	Metric	Imperial	American
Jerusalem artichokes, peeled	450 g	1 lb	1 lb
Potatoes, peeled	225 g	8 oz	½ lb
Salt and pepper			
Water	750 ml	1½ pt	3 cups
Freshly chopped parsley			
Yoghurt	2 tbsp	2 tbsp	2 tbsp

Put the artichokes and potatoes into a saucepan with salt and pepper to taste. Add water and boil until the vegetables are soft.

Put into a blender and liquidize. Pour back into a saucepan and reheat. Add parsley and yoghurt just before serving. Serve in individual soup bowls.

Note: This is a very filling soup and makes an ideal starter with fish to follow.

Total time: 45 mins.

WATERCRESS SOUP

	Metric	Imperial	American
Bunch of watercress	1	1	1
Potatoes, peeled	350 g	12 oz	¾ lb
Water	300 ml	½ pt	1¼ cups
Milk	300 ml	½ pt	1¼ cups
Salt and pepper			
Yoghurt	2 tbsp	2 tbsp	2 tbsp

Wash the watercress thoroughly, cut off the stalks and remove any yellow leaves. Boil the potatoes in salted water till tender. Add watercress, milk, salt and pepper. Boil one minute, then cool. Liquidize in a blender, then reheat. Pour into individual soup bowls and add a ½ tbsp of yoghurt to each before serving.

Total time: 45 mins.

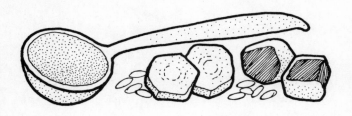

CUCUMBER CUP

	Metric	Imperial	American
Yoghurt	600 ml	1 pt	2½ cups
Cucumber, grated	1 tbsp	1 tbsp	1 tbsp
Clove garlic, crushed	1	1	1
Freshly chopped parsley or chives			
Rosemary	1 pinch	1 pinch	1 pinch
Thyme	1 pinch	1 pinch	1 pinch
Salt			

Put the yoghurt in a mixing bowl. Add the other ingredients and mix well. Chill in refrigerator.
    Serve in small ceramic or glass bowls.

Total time: 10 mins.

MUSHROOM SOUP

	Metric	Imperial	American
Water	1 tbsp	1 tbsp	1 tbsp
Mushrooms, washed and sliced	225 ml	8 oz	½ lb
Salt and pepper			
Basic white sauce (Page 16)	750 ml	1½ pt	3 cups
Dry white wine (optional)	300 ml	½ pt	1¼ cups
Yoghurt			

Put the water into a frying pan. Add the mushrooms and salt and pepper to taste. Cover and simmer for a few minutes until the mushrooms are tender.

Prepare the white sauce. Stir the mushrooms and wine into the sauce and adjust seasoning. Simmer for one minute.

Pour into individual soup bowls, adding a heaped teaspoon of yoghurt to each bowl just before serving.

Total time: 15 mins.

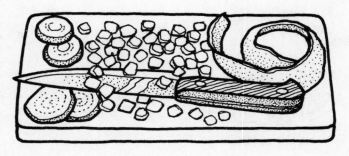

TOMATO SOUP

	Metric	Imperial	American
Flour	2 tbsp	2 tbsp	2 tbsp
Meat stock (Page 14) or water	750 ml	1½ pt	3 cups
Condensed tomato purée	150 g	5 oz	150 g
Onion, peeled and grated	1	1	1
Vinegar	½ tbsp	½ tbsp	½ tbsp
Salt and pepper			
Sugar	1 tbsp	1 tbsp	1 tbsp
Yoghurt	2 tbsp	2 tbsp	2 tbsp

Blend the flour in a little of the liquid until smooth. Pour into a saucepan and heat gently, gradually stirring in the rest of the liquid. When thickened, simmer for several minutes.

Add all the remaining ingredients, except the yoghurt. Stir well and thin to desired consistency with water. Reheat and pour into individual soup bowls, adding a ½ tbsp of yoghurt to each just before serving.

Note: If you like, add a pinch of basil; this accentuates the flavour of the tomatoes.

Total time: 20 mins.

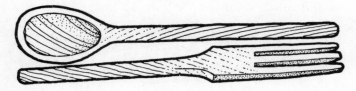

SUMMER CUP

	Metric	Imperial	American
Tomatoes, peeled and de-seeded OR	450 g	1 lb	1 lb
Can of peeled tomatoes	1	1	1
Spring onions, peeled OR	4	4	4
Small onion, peeled	1	1	1
Green pepper, de-seeded	1	1	1
Clove garlic, crushed	1	1	1
Slices of bread	2	2	2
Cucumber	½	½	½
Sugar	½ tbsp	½ tbsp	½ tbsp
Salt and pepper			
Juice of lemon	1	1	1
Freshly chopped basil			

Put the tomatoes, onions, green pepper, garlic, bread and half the cucumber into a blender. Add sugar, salt, pepper and the lemon juice and liquidize. Pour into a serving dish and add basil to taste.

Chop the remainder of the cucumber into small cubes and add to the dish. Chill well.

Note: This Summer Cup looks lovely served in brandy glasses.

Total time: 30 mins.

VEGETABLE POTPOURRI

	Metric	Imperial	American
Meat or chicken stock (Pages 13-14)	750 ml	1½ pt	3 cups
Large carrots, peeled and sliced	2	2	2
Small onions, peeled	2	2	2
Leek, washed and chopped	1	1	1
Potatoes, peeled and diced	2	2	2
Freshly chopped parsley and marjoram			
Salt and pepper			
Worcestershire sauce (optional)			

Put the stock into a saucepan, add the vegetables, herbs, and salt and pepper to taste. Bring to the boil and simmer gently for about 30 minutes. Check that the onions have disintegrated. If not, break up with the back of a spoon.

Serve hot with strips of crisp toast. If you like, add a few drops of Worcestershire sauce.

Total time: 40 mins.

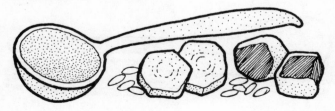

MIXED VEGETABLE SOUP

	Metric	Imperial	American
Large potatoes, peeled	2	2	2
Large carrots, peeled	2	2	2
Large leeks, washed and trimmed	2	2	2
Large onion, peeled	1	1	1
Bay leaf	1	1	1
Salt and pepper			
Yoghurt	2 tbsp	2 tbsp	2 tbsp
Freshly chopped parsley			

Put all the vegetables, with the bay leaf, into a pressure cooker, cover with water and season with salt and pepper. Cook at H pressure for about 20 minutes.

Leave the vegetables and liquid to cool, then pour into a blender and liquidize until smooth. Reheat.

Just before serving, add the yoghurt and sprinkle with chopped parsley. Mix well and serve hot.

Total time: 35 mins.

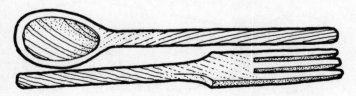

STARTERS

PRAWN COCKTAIL*

	Metric	Imperial	American
Lettuce	1	1	1
Cucumber, sliced	¼	¼	¼
Pink salad dressing (Page 120)	300 ml	½ pt	1¼ cups
Prawns, cooked and peeled	225 g	8 oz	½lb

Slice the lettuce into fine strips and cut the cucumber into small cubes. Line individual dishes or glasses with the lettuce, pile prawns into the centre of each and decorate with cucumber.

Prepare the pink salad dressing and pour over the prawns. Chill. Serve with thin slices of brown bread, and a dish of chive whip (Page 124).

Total time: 10 mins.

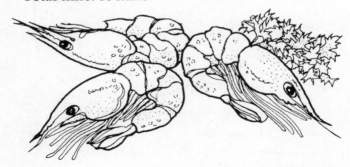

SHRIMP BOATS*

	Metric	Imperial	American
Hard boiled eggs	2	2	2
Shrimps or prawns, cooked and peeled	100 g	4 oz	¼ lb
Tomatoes, sliced	2	2	2
Pink salad dressing (Page 120)	300 ml	½ pt	1¼ cups
Cucumber slices	4	4	4

Shell the eggs and cut them in half lengthways. Scoop out the yolks, then fill the egg whites with shrimps or prawns. Place on individual small plates with slices of tomato.

Prepare the pink salad dressing and pour over each boat. Decorate with an upright slice of cucumber.

Serve chilled, with slices of brown bread, and a cheese whip (Pages 122-5) for spreading.

Total time: 15 mins.

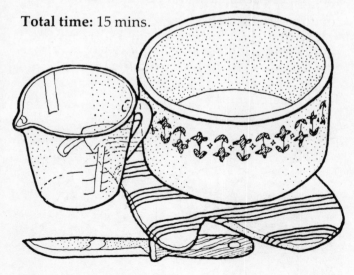

TOMATO JELLY

	Metric	Imperial	American
Aspic powder	1 pkt	1 pkt	1 pkt
Can of tomato juice	450 g	1 lb	1 lb
Juice of lemon	½	½	½
Worcestershire sauce	5 drops	5 drops	5 drops
White wine (optional)	2 tbsp	2 tbsp	2 tbsp
Salt			
Green pepper	1	1	1

Dissolve the aspic as directed on the packet, using hot tomato juice instead of water. Then make up the required quantity with the rest of the tomato juice, lemon juice and Worcestershire sauce. Replace some lemon juice with wine, if desired. Season with a little salt and mix well. Pour into a jelly ring or pudding basin and leave to cool and set.

When set, stand the ring or basin in warm water for a moment to loosen the jelly. Turn out on to a serving dish.

Cut the green pepper open and remove the pith and pips. Slice thinly and place around the jelly. Serve cold.

Note: This makes a simple but delicious starter on a summer day.

Total time: 15 mins, plus setting time.

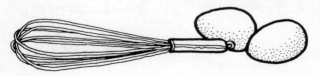

TOP HAT TOMATOES

	Metric	Imperial	American
Large tomatoes	4	4	4
Cottage cheese	4 tbsp	4 tbsp	4 tbsp
Clove garlic, peeled and crushed OR	1	1	1
Freshly chopped chives	½ tbsp	½ tbsp	½ tbsp
Salt			
Lettuce leaves			

Slice the tops off the tomatoes with a sharp knife, and scoop out the seeds.

Mix the cottage cheese with the garlic or chopped chives and salt. Stuff the tomatoes with this mixture, forming a dome at the top of each tomato. Replace the tomato tops, and chill in the refrigerator. Serve on individual small plates on a bed of lettuce leaves.

Total time: 20 mins.

Note: This pâté will keep in the refrigerator for up to a week. If you like mushrooms, you can also slice 100 g/4 oz/¼ lb unpeeled mushrooms, and cook them with the liver and onion.

Total time: 1 hour.

NOTE ON PANCAKES

Pancakes are very versatile since they can be used as a starter, a sweet or even as a main course with savoury fillings.

If you put the filled pancakes into a covered ovenproof dish, you can keep them hot for a limited time in the oven at a very low temperature.

BASIC PANCAKES

	Metric	Imperial	American
Self-raising flour	115 g	4 oz	1 cup
Milk	300 ml	½ pt	1¼ cups
Egg	1	1	1
Salt			

Sieve the flour into a mixing bowl. Stir in the milk, egg and salt to taste. The consistency of the batter should be like salad cream. If necessary, add a little water to thin.

Heat a frying pan until a few drops of water sprinkled into it sizzle and evaporate. Turn the heat down to low. Ladle enough of the pancake mix into the pan to cover the bottom thinly, and cook until the edges curl up. Turn over and cook the other side in the same way.

Put the pancake on to a pre-warmed ovenproof dish to keep warm while you cook the rest of the batter.

Total time: 30 mins.

CHEESE AND TOMATO PANCAKES

	Metric	Imperial	American
Basic pancake batter (Page 44)			
Curd or cottage cheese	225 g	8 oz	½ lb
Freshly chopped chives			
Salt and pepper			
Tomatoes, sliced	2	2	2

Make the basic pancakes.

Mix the cheese with chives and salt and pepper. Spread the cheese on each pancake and add the tomato slices. Roll up.

Put into an ovenproof dish and heat in a pre-heated oven (200°C/400°F/Gas mark 6) for at least 10 minutes.

Note: These pancakes can be served hot or cold.

Total time: 40 mins.

ASPARAGUS AND CHEESE PANCAKES

	Metric	Imperial	American
Basic pancake batter (Page 44)			
Small can asparagus tips	1	1	1
Salt			
Curd or cottage cheese	225 g	8 oz	½ lb

Make the basic pancakes.

Turn out the asparagus tips and drain off all the liquid. Mix the cheese with a little salt. Spread the cheese on each pancake. Add the asparagus tips, and roll each pancake up.

Put into an ovenproof dish and reheat in a preheated oven 180°F/350°F/Gas mark 4 for 15 minutes.

Note: These pancakes can also be served cold.

Total time: 45 mins.

MUSHROOM PANCAKES

	Metric	Imperial	American
Basic pancake batter (Page 44)			
Water	2 tbsp	2 tbsp	2 tbsp
Mushrooms, washed and sliced	225 g	8 oz	½ lb
Salt and pepper			
Freshly chopped herbs			

Make the basic pancake batter.

Put the water in a frying pan, add the mushrooms and season with salt and pepper. Cover and simmer for 3 minutes. Drain off the water. Add a few fresh herbs.

Spread the mushrooms on each pancake as you make them, fold over, and put into an ovenproof dish. Reheat in oven at 350°F/180°C/Gas mark 4. Serve piping hot.

Total time: 35 mins.

SPINACH PANCAKES

	Metric	Imperial	American
Basic pancake batter (Page 44)			
Spinach	450 g	1 lb	1 lb
Salt and pepper			

Make the basic pancake batter.

Cook the spinach, add salt and pepper, and chop finely or liquidize in a blender. Drain well.

Cook one pancake, fill it with a heaped tablespoon of spinach, fold over and keep very hot on an ovenproof dish. Continue cooking the pancakes, filling each one in the same way. Serve piping hot as a starter.

Total time: 30 mins.

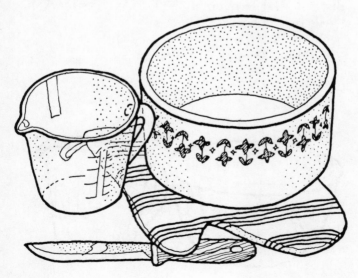

FISH AND SHELLFISH

RED MULLET IN SALT

	Metric	Imperial	American
Coarse sea salt	450 g	1 lb	1 lb
Whole red mullet OR	1	1	1
Small mullets	4	4	4
Freshly chopped parsley			

Spread half the sea salt on the bottom of an ovenproof dish. Clean the fish, place it whole on the salt, then completely cover the fish with a thick layer of salt.

Bake in a preheated 400°F/200°C/Gas mark 6 oven for about 45 minutes. Peel off the hardened salt from the top, garnish the fish with parsley and serve hot with boiled potatoes and salad.

Total time: 50 mins.

FILLETS OF PLAICE WITH MUSHROOMS

	Metric	Imperial	American
Fillets of plaice, skinned	8	8	8
Salt and freshly ground black pepper			
Juice of lemon	½	½	½
Mushrooms, washed and sliced	225 g	8 oz	½ lb
Freshly chopped parsley			

Put the fillets into a large ovenproof dish and sprinkle with salt and lemon juice.

Season the mushrooms with a little salt and freshly ground black pepper and add to the dish with the fish. Cover with a lid or kitchen foil, and bake in a preheated 400°F/200°C/Gas mark 6 oven for 35 minutes. Sprinkle with freshly ground black pepper and garnish with parsley.

Serve with mashed potatoes and spinach.

Total time: 45 mins.

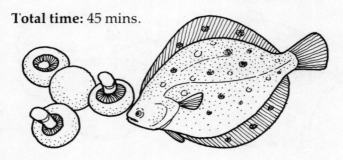

CURRIED PRAWNS*

	Metric	Imperial	American
Flour	2 tbsp	2 tbsp	2 tbsp
Water or fish stock	600 ml	1 pint	2½ cups
Juice of lemon	½	½	½
Onion, peeled and grated	½	½	½
Apple, grated	1	1	1
Curry powder	½ tbsp	½ tbsp	½ tbsp
Sugar	1 tbsp	1 tbsp	1 tbsp
Sultanas	1 tbsp	1 tbsp	1 tbsp
Salt			
Prawns, cooked and peeled	350 g	12 oz	¾ lb

Blend the flour in a saucepan with a little water or stock to a smooth paste. Then add the water or fish stock and lemon juice, stirring all the time. Add all the other ingredients, except the prawns. Simmer for 10 minutes, stirring all the time. Stir in the prawns and reheat. Serve hot with long grain rice.

Note: Instead of prawns, cooked fish, such as skinned and boned cod or haddock, may be used. The fish cooking water can be used as stock.

Total time: 35 mins.

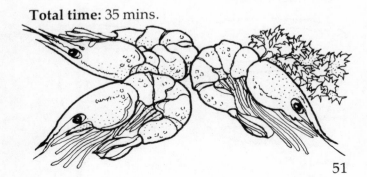

51

BAKED HADDOCK FILLETS WITH TOMATOES

	Metric	Imperial	American
Haddock fillets (fresh or frozen), skinned	4	4	4
Juice of lemon	½	½	½
Salt			
Tomatoes	8	8	8
Shallots, peeled and finely chopped	2	2	2
Pepper			

Place the haddock fillets in a large casserole and sprinkle with lemon juice and salt.

Plunge the tomatoes into boiling water for one minute, then skin and halve them and arrange around the fish. Sprinkle the shallots over the tomatoes and season with a little salt and pepper.

Place the casserole in the 400°F/200°C/Gas mark 6 oven and bake for about 30 minutes (45 minutes if frozen). Serve with rice or potatoes.

Total time: 40 mins.

POACHED HADDOCK FILLETS

	Metric	Imperial	American
Haddock fillets, skinned	700 g	1½ lb	1½ lb
Water	2 tbsp	2 tbsp	2 tbsp
Small onion, peeled and sliced	1	1	1
Juice of lemon	½	½	½
Salt and pepper			
Sauce piquante (Page 21)	300 ml	½ pt	1¼ cups

Put the haddock fillets in a frying pan with the water. Cover with slices of onion and sprinkle with lemon juice, salt and pepper. Cover and simmer for about 20 minutes (35 minutes if the fish is frozen).

Meanwhile, prepare the sauce piquante.

When the fish is ready put into a warmed dish. Serve with the sauce piquante, boiled potatoes, and a salad or hot vegetables.

Total time: 30 mins.

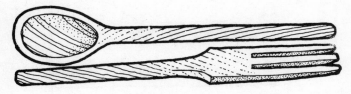

BAKED HADDOCK FILLETS

	Metric	Imperial	American
Small onion, peeled and sliced	1	1	1
Haddock fillets (fresh or frozen), skinned	700 g	1½ lb	1½ lb
Salt			
Juice of lemon	½	½	½
Paprika or freshly chopped chives			

Line the bottom of a casserole with the onion slices. Place the haddock on top of the onion, sprinkle with salt and lemon juice, and cover.

Put the casserole into the preheated 400°F/ 200°C/Gas mark 6 oven and bake for about 20 minutes (or 35 minutes if frozen). Sprinkle with paprika or chopped chives. Serve immediately with potatoes and a spinach purée.

Total time: 30 mins.

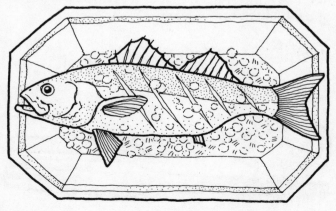

HADDOCK FILLETS ON A BED OF SPINACH

	Metric	Imperial	American
Spinach	700 g	1½ lb	1½ lb
Salt and pepper			
Haddock fillets (fresh or frozen), skinned	4	4	4
Juice of lemon	½	½	½
Cheese sauce (Page 20)	600 ml	1 pt	2½ cups

Put the spinach into a saucepan with two tablespoons of water. Season with salt and pepper, cover and bring quickly to the boil for about 1 minute, then drain and put into a casserole.

Place the haddock fillets on top of the spinach and sprinkle with a little salt and lemon juice.

Make the cheese sauce and pour over the fish. Bake in a preheated 200°C/400°F/Gas mark 6 oven for 30 minutes (or 45 minutes if frozen). Serve hot with boiled new potatoes.

Total time: 30 mins.

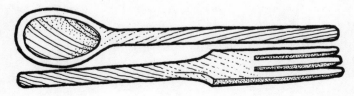

BAKED HADDOCK FILLETS WITH GRAPEFRUIT

	Metric	Imperial	American
Haddock fillets (fresh or frozen), skinned	700 g	1½ lb	1½ lb
Juice of lemon	½	½	½
Salt			
Grapefruit, thinly sliced	1	1	1
Cornflour	1 tbsp	1 tbsp	1 tbsp
Brown sugar	1 tbsp	1 tbsp	1 tbsp
Grapefruit juice	150 ml	¼ pt	⅔ cup

Put the haddock fillets into a flat ovenproof dish. Sprinkle with lemon juice and salt. Cut grapefruit into thin slices but do not remove the peel. Top the fillets with thin slices of grapefruit. Cover the dish with a lid or kitchen foil and bake in a preheated 200°C/400°F/Gas mark 6 oven for about 20 minutes (35 minutes if frozen).

Drain off the liquid into a saucepan, place over a low heat, add the cornflour and blend to a smooth paste. Stir in the sugar, a pinch of salt and grapefruit juice, and bring to the boil, stirring all the time. Simmer for several minutes then pour over the fish.

Serve with rice and salad or celery hearts.

Total time: 30 mins.

COD FILLETS WITH MUSHROOMS

	Metric	Imperial	American
Cod fillets (fresh or frozen), skinned	4	4	4
Salt and pepper			
Juice of lemon	½	½	½
Mushrooms, washed and sliced	225 g	8 oz	½ lb
Basic white sauce (Page 16)	600 ml	1 pt	2½ cups

Place the cod fillets in a casserole and sprinkle with salt, pepper and lemon juice.

Season the mushrooms with a little salt and pepper and add to the casserole. Cover and cook in a preheated 400°F/200°C/Gas mark 6 oven for 30 minutes (or 45 if frozen).

Meanwhile prepare the white sauce.

When the fillets are cooked, pour the white sauce on top and serve hot, with rice and broad beans, or any other vegetables.

Total time: 35 mins.

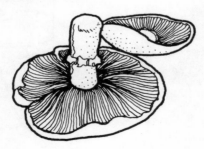

COD FILLETS IN CHEESE SAUCE

	Metric	Imperial	American
Cheese sauce (Page 13)	350 ml	¾ pt	2 cups
Cod fillets, washed and skinned	900 g	2 lb	2 lb
Mushrooms, washed and sliced	175 g	6 oz	1½ cups
Salt and pepper			
White wine (optional)	1 tbsp	1 tbsp	1 tbsp

Make the cheese sauce.

Put the cod fillets into an ovenproof dish and cover with the mushrooms. Season with salt and pepper. Pour the cheese sauce on top, add the wine and cook in a preheated 375°F/190°C/Gas mark 5 oven for about 20 minutes. Serve with new potatoes and a spinach purée.

Total time: 30 mins.

DOVER SOLE

	Metric	Imperial	American
Fillets of Dover sole, skinned	8	8	8
Salt			
Juice of lemon	1	1	1
Water	1 tbsp	1 tbsp	1 tbsp
White wine (optional)	150 ml	1/4 pt	2/3 cup
Cheese sauce (Page 20)	600 ml	1 pt	2 1/2 cups

Put the fillets into a frying pan. Sprinkle with salt and either lemon juice or wine and add water. Cover and simmer for 10 to 15 minutes, depending on the thickness of the fillets.

Meanwhile prepare the cheese sauce, replacing some of the liquid with the rest of the white wine or lemon juice.

When the fillets are cooked, place them in an oblong serving dish, and pour the hot cheese sauce on top, or serve separately in a sauceboat.

Serve with new potatoes and French beans.

Total time: 20 mins.

DOVER SOLE WITH SHRIMPS*

	Metric	Imperial	American
Fillets of Dover sole (two per person), skinned	8	8	8
Salt			
Juice of lemon	1	1	1
Shrimps, cooked and peeled	225 g	8 oz	½ lb
Basic white sauce (Page 16)	600 ml	1 pt	2½ cups
Freshly chopped parsley			

Sprinkle the fillets with salt and a little of the lemon juice. Put a few shrimps on each fillet, then roll up and secure with a small wooden skewer or toothpick.

Place all the rolled fillets in a casserole, add half the rest of the lemon juice, cover with a lid, and cook in a preheated 400°F/200°/Gas mark 6 oven for 30 minutes.

Meanwhile prepare the white sauce and season with the remaining lemon juice and chopped parsley.

Pour the white sauce over the cooked fillets and serve hot with rice or potatoes and French beans.

Total time: 30 mins.

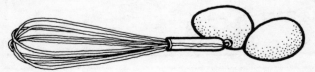

RAINBOW TROUT IN FOIL

	Metric	Imperial	American
Rainbow trout (per person)	1	1	1
Salt			
Freshly chopped parsley or chives			
Juice of lemon	1	1	1

Cut out pieces of foil large enough to wrap each fish separately. Place each trout on to foil, sprinkle with salt inside and insert the parsley or the chives. Sprinkle with lemon juice. Add two teaspoons of water and wrap foil round the trout. Do not double wrap.

Place the fish in a roasting tin and cook in a preheated 375°F/190°C/Gas mark 5 oven for 20 minutes.

Serve in the foil on warmed plates, and provide a dish for the foil when the fish is unwrapped. Serve with boiled potatoes and mixed salad.

Note: For best results with frozen trout, defrost completely before cooking (2 to 3 hours at room temperature).

Total time: 25 mins.

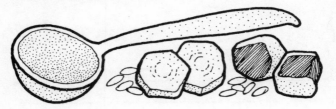

TRUITE BLEUE

	Metric	Imperial	American
Trout (per person)	1	1	1
Vinegar	1 tbsp	1 tbsp	1 tbsp
Salt			
Peppercorns	6	6	6
Mixed spices	1 tsp	1 tsp	1 tsp

Pour just enough water into a large saucepan to cover the fish. Add the vinegar and a little salt, the peppercorns and the mixed spices. Bring to the boil then add the trout.

Reduce the heat and simmer lightly for about 15 minutes until the fish eyes turn to white balls.

With a fish slice carefully put the trout on an oblong dish. Serve immediately with new potatoes sprinkled with chopped parsley.

Total time: 20 mins.

GRILLED RAINBOW TROUT

	Metric	Imperial	American
Rainbow trout (per person)	1	1	1
Salt			
Freshly chopped parsley or chives			
Juice of lemon	½	½	½
Lemon, sliced	1	1	1

Sprinkle the trout inside with salt and insert the herbs. Add a little lemon juice.

Place the trout in the bottom of a grill pan and sprinkle with salt and lemon juice. Place under preheated grill, and cook for 4 minutes at highest temperature, then reduce to medium heat and cook for another 6 minutes, turning the fish to cook equally on both sides.

Place the cooked trout on a prewarmed dish and pour the juices from the grill pan on top. Garnish with slices of lemon. Serve with new potatoes or thick slices of brown toast and spinach purée.

Note: For best results when using frozen trout, defrost completely before cooking (2 to 3 hours at room temperature).

Total time: 30 mins.

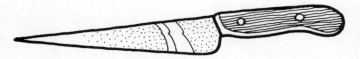

POACHED RAINBOW TROUT

	Metric	Imperial	American
Rainbow trout (per person)	1	1	1
Salt			
Freshly chopped parsley or chives			
Juice of lemon OR	1	1	1
Dry white wine (optional)	1 tbsp	1 tbsp	1 tbsp

Sprinkle the trout inside and out with salt. Insert the parsley or chives.

Cover the bottom of a frying pan with a little water, add either the lemon juice or the wine and sprinkle with salt. Bring to the boil, add the trout, cover the pan and simmer for 15 to 20 minutes, depending on the size of the trout. The trout is ready when the eyes look like white balls.

Place on a warmed dish and garnish with parsley or thin cucumber slices. Serve with boiled or jacket potatoes.

Note: For best results with frozen trout, defrost completely before cooking (2 to 3 hours at room temperature).

Total time: 20 mins.

MAIN COURSES

ROAST CHICKEN

	Metric	Imperial	American
Chicken	1.5 kg	3 lb	3 lb
Salt and pepper			
Brown gravy			
(Page 15)			
Red wine (optional)			

Season the chicken inside and out with salt and pepper, and put on a trivet or wire tray in a roasting pan. (The fat will then drip into the tin during roasting and not be absorbed by the bird.) Cover with foil. Roast in oven for 20 minutes per lb, plus 20 minutes at 400°F/200°C/Gas mark 6. Remove roasted chicken from trivet and place on carving dish.

Meanwhile, prepare the gravy, using red wine to replace some stock, if desired.

Serve hot with rice or potatoes and vegetables.

Note: There will be fat and juice left in the bottom of the roasting pan. Pour this into a bowl and let it cool. Remove the fat which forms on the surface and store the juice for further use in the freezer.

Total time: 1 hr 20 mins.

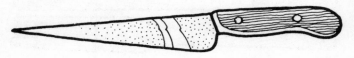

CHICKEN CASSEROLE

	Metric	Imperial	American
Chicken OR	1.5 kg	3 lb	3 lb
Chicken joints	4	4	4
Salt and pepper			
Basic white sauce			
(Page 16)	600 ml	1 pt	2½ cups
Bouquet garni			
Yoghurt	1 tbsp	1 tbsp	1 tbsp
Juice of lemon	½	½	½

Put the chicken or chicken joints on the trivet in a pressure cooker and season with salt and pepper. Add water to trivet level and cook at H pressure for 30 minutes. When cooked remove the skin and bones, cut the meat into neat pieces and put into a casserole.

Meanwhile, make the white sauce, adding bouquet garni. When almost ready, stir in yoghurt and lemon juice to taste. Remove the bouquet garni.

Serve with rice, carrots and celery hearts.

Note: For freezing add lemon juice and yoghurt only when reheating.

Total time: 1 hr 10 mins.

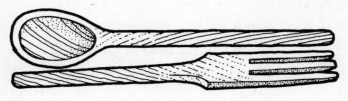

CHICKEN
À LA KING

	Metric	Imperial	American
Chicken	1.5 kg	3 lb	3 lb
Salt and pepper			
Mixed herbs or bouquet garni			
Basic white sauce (Page 16)	600 ml	1 pt	2½ cups
Mushrooms, washed and sliced	225 g	8 oz	½ lb
Yoghurt	2 tbsp	2 tbsp	2 tbsp

Wipe the chicken and place it on the trivet in a pressure cooker. Season with a little salt and pepper. Add water to trivet level and mixed herbs or bouquet garni. Cook for one hour at H pressure.

Meanwhile, make the white sauce.

Put the mushrooms into a frying pan with two tablespoons of water. Season with a little salt, cover and simmer for about 3 minutes.

Remove the chicken from the pressure cooker, skin and bone it and cut the meat into neat cubes. (Keep the skin and bones to make stock.)

Put the meat into a casserole. Mix the mushrooms and their liquid with the white sauce and pour over the chicken.

Cover the casserole and put in a preheated oven to heat through. Stir in the yoghurt just before serving. Serve with rice and cauliflower, or broccoli.

Total time: 1½ hrs.

CHICKEN PÂTÉ

	Metric	Imperial	American
Chicken joints	3	3	3
Salt and pepper			
Mushrooms, washed and sliced	100 g	4 oz	¼ lb
Freshly chopped parsley	1 tbsp	1 tbsp	1 tbsp
Slices of brown bread	2	2	2
Yoghurt	300 ml	½ pt	1¼ cups
Juice of lemon	½	½	½
Tomato purée	1 tbsp	1 tbsp	1 tbsp

Place the chicken joints on the trivet in a pressure cooker and season with salt and pepper. Add water to trivet level and cook for 15 minutes at H pressure.

Meanwhile, put the mushrooms into a frying pan with two tablespoons of water and a little salt. Cover and simmer for about 3 minutes until tender.

Remove the cooked chicken joints from the pressure cooker and skin and bone them. Put the chicken meat through a mincer with the parsley and mushrooms and finally the bread.

Put the mixture into a casserole or tureen, add the yoghurt, lemon juice and the tomato purée. Mix well, then stand the casserole or tureen in a *bain-marie* and put it into a preheated 400°F/200°C/ Gas mark 6 oven to cook for 45 minutes.

Serve either cold as a starter, with toast or crispbread, or hot as a main dish with vegetables.

Total time: 1 hr 10 mins.

CHICKEN CATALÁN

	Metric	Imperial	American
Chicken joints	4	4	4
Salt			
Onion, peeled and sliced	1	1	1
Sweet paprika	1 tbsp	1 tbsp	1 tbsp
Green peppers, de-seeded and sliced	2	2	2
Tomatoes, peeled and halved	225 g	8 oz	½ lb
White wine (optional)	3 tbsp	3 tbsp	3 tbsp
Tomato purée	1 tbsp	1 tbsp	1 tbsp

Place chicken joints on the trivet in a pressure cooker, season with salt and add water to level of trivet. Cook for 20 minutes at H pressure.

Meanwhile, put the onion, paprika, green peppers and tomatoes into a frying pan and season. Add two tablespoons of water, cover and simmer for 20 minutes. Add white wine and tomato purée and mix well.

Skin cooked chicken portions and place in a casserole. Pour the vegetables on top. Cover, reheat in oven and serve with rice.

Total time: 30 mins.

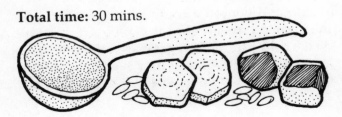

CHICKEN CURRY

	Metric	Imperial	American
Chicken joints	4	4	4
Salt			
Carrots, peeled and sliced	2	2	2
Onions, peeled and sliced	2	2	2
Cooking apples, peeled and sliced	2	2	2
Flour	1 tbsp	1 tbsp	1 tbsp
Curry powder	1½ tbsp	1½ tbsp	1½ tbsp
Brown sugar	1 tbsp	1 tbsp	1 tbsp
Vinegar	½ tbsp	½ tbsp	½ tbsp
Pineapple chunks	225 g	8 oz	½ lb

Put the chicken joints on the trivet in a pressure cooker, and season with a little salt. Add salted water to trivet level and cook at H pressure for 30 minutes.

Meanwhile, cook the carrots and onions in a little salted water until tender, add the apples and simmer for another minute or two. Strain, keeping the liquid. Blend the flour, curry powder, brown sugar and vinegar in a saucepan, add a little of the vegetable cooking liquid and make a smooth paste. Slowly add the rest of the liquid, then simmer, stirring all the time, until the mixture thickens.

Skin and bone the cooked chicken joints, cut the meat into small cubes and put into a casserole dish. Add strained vegetables and pineapple chunks. Cover with the curry sauce and put the casserole into a preheated 400°F/200°C/Gas mark

6 oven to heat through. Serve with rice.

Total time: 45 mins.

CHICKEN RISOTTO

	Metric	Imperial	American
Chicken joints	2	2	2
Salt			
Rice	350 g	12 oz	2 cups
Saffron	1 pinch	1 pinch	1 pinch
Carrots, peeled and diced	3	3	3
Peas, shelled	175 g	6 oz	⅔ cup

Put the chicken joints on the trivet in a pressure cooker, add water to trivet level, season with salt, and cook for 20 minutes at H pressure.

Meanwhile put the rice into a saucepan, season with salt and add the saffron. Cover with 3 times its volume of boiling water and simmer over a low heat until all the water is absorbed.

Skin and bone the chicken and cut the meat into small pieces.

Cook the carrots and peas in a little salted water until tender.

Put the cooked rice, meat and vegetables into an ovenproof dish and mix well. Cover and put the dish into a preheated 400°F/200°C/Gas mark 6 oven to heat thoroughly for 15 minutes.

Note: This is a very filling dish and should be followed by a light sweet, such as stewed fruit or jelly.

Total time: 50 mins.

CURRIED VEAL

	Metric	Imperial	American
Lean veal	700 g	1½ lb	1½ lb
Salt			
Carrots, peeled and sliced	4	4	4
Large onions, peeled and sliced	2	2	2
Salted water	250 ml	½ pt	1¼ cups
Large cooking apple, peeled and sliced	1	1	1
Curry powder	1½ tbsp	1½ tbsp	1½ tbsp
Cornflour	½ tbsp	½ tbsp	½ tbsp
Brown sugar	1 tbsp	1 tbsp	1 tbsp
Vinegar	1 tbsp	1 tbsp	1 tbsp
Sultanas	175 g	6 oz	⅔ cup

Trim all the fat off the veal, then cut into small chunks and season with salt. Put the meat on the trivet in a pressure cooker and add salted water to trivet level. Cook at H pressure for 35 minutes.

Meanwhile, put the carrots and onions into a saucepan with the salted water. Cook until tender, then add the apple. Simmer for another few minutes.

Put the curry powder, cornflour, sugar and vinegar into a saucepan and season with salt. Add a little of the vegetable cooking liquid and mix to a smooth paste. Simmer over a low heat, stirring all the time, adding enough of the remaining vegetable liquid to get a smooth consistency. Add the sultanas.

Put the cooked meat and all the vegetables into a preheated casserole and coat with the curry sauce. Cover and reheat in a 400°F/200°C/Gas mark 6 oven for about 20 minutes.

Serve hot with a bowl of rice and a small dish of chutney.

Total time: 55 mins.

VEAL ROULADE

	Metric	Imperial	American
Mushroom sauce (Page 18)	375 ml	¾ pint	2 cups
Veal escalopes	4	4	4
Salt and pepper			
Sage leaves	4	4	4
Mushrooms, peeled and finely chopped	100 g	4 oz	¼ lb
Juice of lemon	½	½	½

Make the mushroom sauce.

Flatten the veal slices to an even thickness and season with salt and pepper. Place one sage leaf on each slice. Spread the mushrooms over the veal, roll up each slice and fasten with a wooden skewer or toothpick, then sprinkle with lemon juice. Place the veal roulades in an ovenproof dish and pour the mushroom sauce on top. Cover and put into the preheated 400°F/200°C/Gas mark 6 oven for about 40 minutes.

Serve hot with rice or potatoes. Carrots and peas go well with this dish both in taste and appearance.

Total time: 50 mins.

CASSEROLE OF VEAL

	Metric	Imperial	American
Veal	700 g	1½ lb	1½ lb
Salt			
Onion, peeled and chopped	1	1	1
Carrot, peeled and chopped	1	1	1
Small clove garlic, chopped	1	1	1
Pepper			
Freshly chopped rosemary or thyme			
Juice of lemon OR	1	1	1
White wine (optional)	150 ml	¼ pt	⅔ cup
Hot water	300 ml	½ pt	1¼ cups
Basic white sauce (Page 16)	600 ml	1 pt	2½ cups
Yoghurt	2 tbsp	2 tbsp	2 tbsp

Remove any fat from the veal, then sprinkle with a little salt. Put one tablespoon of water into a hot frying pan, add the meat, reduce heat to medium and quickly turn it to seal on all sides. Put in an ovenproof casserole.

Add the onion, carrot and garlic to the casserole. Season with salt and pepper. Add a pinch of rosemary or thyme with the hot water, and cover.

Place casserole in a preheated 450°F/230°C/Gas mark 8 oven and cook for 40 minutes.

Meanwhile, prepare the white sauce, add white wine or the lemon juice. Keep warm.

Take the meat out of the oven, strain off the juice for future use, and discard the vegetables.

Cover the meat with the white sauce and put the casserole back into the oven for a few minutes to reheat. Before serving, stir in the yoghurt. Serve hot with flat noodles and any vegetables in season.

Total time: 1 hr.

HUNGARIAN PAPRIKA

	Metric	Imperial	American
Veal	700 g	1½ lb	1½ lb
Salt			
Sweet paprika	1 tbsp	1 tbsp	1 tbsp
Basic white sauce (Page 16)	600 ml	1 pt	2½ cups
Onion, peeled and cut into rings	1	1	1

Remove all traces of fat from the veal, then cut the meat into small chunks. Put into a pressure cooker and toss over medium heat to seal. Remove from pressure cooker. Put the trivet into the pressure cooker and add salted water to trivet level. Sprinkle the meat with salt and half the paprika and place on the trivet. Cook for 25 minutes at H pressure.

While the meat is cooking, prepare the white sauce and keep hot.

Put the onion rings into a frying pan with 3 tablespoons of water and simmer over a low heat until the rings glaze. Add salt and the rest of the paprika. Stir in the white sauce and mix well. Keep hot.

When the meat is cooked put it into a casserole, pour the paprika sauce on top, cover and heat in a preheated oven.

Serve hot with rice or boiled potatoes.

Total time: 1 hr.

VEAL STEW

	Metric	Imperial	American
Stewing veal	700 g	1½ lb	1½ lb
Salt and pepper			
Rosemary	1 sprig	1 sprig	1 sprig
Mushrooms, washed and sliced	100 g	4 oz	¼ lb
Basic white sauce (Page 16)	600 ml	1 pt	2½ cups
Juice of lemon	½	½	½

Cut off all fat from the veal, then cut the meat into cubes and season with salt and pepper. Put the meat on the trivet in a pressure cooker and add salted water to trivet level. Add rosemary. Cook at H pressure for 30 minutes.

Put two tablespoons of water into the frying pan, add the mushrooms, season with salt and pepper, and simmer for about 3 minutes with the lid on.

Prepare the white sauce then add the lemon juice and the mushrooms with their liquid.

Remove the meat from the pressure cooker and put it into a casserole. Add the white sauce and mix well. Put into a preheated oven to heat through.

Serve hot with potatoes, carrots or any other vegetables.

Total time: 45 mins.

ROAST TURKEY

	Metric	Imperial	American
Turkey	3 kg	6 lb	6 lb
Salt			
Cooking apples, peeled, cored and quartered	450 g	1 lb	1 lb
Freshly chopped rosemary			
Brown gravy (Page 15)			
Red wine (optional)			

Wipe the turkey and sprinkle with salt, then stuff with the apples. Put the turkey on a trivet in a roasting pan, sprinkle with rosemary and cover. Roast in oven at 20 minutes per lb (450 g) plus 20 minutes at 425°F/220°C/Gas mark 7.

Remove cooked turkey from trivet and place on a carving dish.

Meanwhile prepare gravy. Use red wine instead of some of the liquid for the gravy if so desired.

Serve hot with baked potatoes and vegetables.

Notes: Retain meat juices from roasting pan for future use.

You could stuff the other end of the bird as well: put 2 slices of brown bread, turkey liver, ¼ onion, and ¼ lb (100 g) rinsed mushrooms through mincer, add salt and pepper to taste, mix well and use to stuff bird. Remember that all stuffing will collect a fair amount of fat from the bird as it roasts. This should not be eaten by anyone on a fat free diet. Serves 6 or more.

Total time: 2½ hrs.

TURKEY STEAKS

	Metric	Imperial	American
Turkey steak (per person)	1	1	1
Salt			
Juice of lemon	½	½	½
Flour	2 tbsp	2 tbsp	2 tbsp
Egg white	1	1	1
Breadcrumbs	4 tbsp	4 tbsp	4 tbsp
Freshly chopped herbs			

Flatten the turkey steaks to an equal thickness, then sprinkle with salt and lemon juice. Dust both sides with flour. Beat the egg white lightly with a fork and dip each turkey steak into it.

Mix the breadcrumbs on a chopping board with the herbs and coat both sides of the steaks, covering them well.

Heat three tablespoons of water in a frying pan. When sizzling add the steaks one by one. Cook each steak on both sides, for about 3 minutes adding a little water if necessary.

Keep the steaks hot on a warmed serving dish. Serve hot with boiled potatoes and fresh vegetables.

Total time: 20 mins.

POTROAST
OF BEEF

	Metric	Imperial	American
Blade steak (preferably eye of blade)	900 g	2 lb	2 lb
Salt and pepper			
Potatoes, peeled and halved	450 g	1 lb	1 lb
Brown gravy (Page 15)			
Red wine (optional)			

Trim any fat off the meat, then sprinkle with salt and pepper and put on a trivet or wire tray in a roasting tin. If there is room, put the potatoes round the meat to roast with it. Add water to just below the trivet or tray. Tightly cover with foil and put into preheated 425°F/220°C/Gas mark 7 oven. Roast for about 1 hour.

Meanwhile, prepare the brown gravy using red wine to replace some of the liquid if so desired. Pour it into a sauceboat and keep hot.

When the meat and potatoes are cooked put them into prewarmed dishes. Serve very hot. Diced carrots and peas go well with it.

Notes: Serves 6. Pour the meat juices from the roasting tin into a bowl, and keep for future use. For a change, sweet and sour sauce (Page 24) could be used instead of brown gravy.

Total time: 1½ hrs.

BEEF STEW IN PRESSURE COOKER

	Metric	Imperial	American
Blade steak prefer-ably (eye of blade)	700 g	1½ lb	1½ lb
Salt and pepper			
Freshly chopped marjoram, parsley and thyme			
Medium size onions, peeled and sliced	2	2	2
Carrots, peeled and sliced	2	2	2
Large leek, washed and sliced	1	1	1
Stick of celery, washed and sliced	1	1	1
Basic brown sauce (Page 17)	600 g	1 pt	2½ cups
Red wine (optional)			

Remove any fat from the steak, cut it into chunks, season and add herbs. Place meat on the trivet in a pressure cooker and add salted water to level of trivet. Cook at H pressure for 45 minutes.

Meanwhile, cook onions, carrots, leek and celery in a little salted water until tender. Drain.

Prepare basic brown sauce using wine to replace some liquid if so desired.

Remove cooked meat from pressure cooker. Place in a preheated casserole. Add the vegetables and gravy and serve with baked potatoes.

Total time: 1 hr.

BUTTOCK STEAK IN PRESSURE COOKER

	Metric	Imperial	American
Buttock steak	1.5 kg	3 lb	3 lb
Salt and pepper			
Brown gravy			
(Page 15)			
Red wine (optional)			

Put the meat into a dry pressure cooker on a medium heat and turn meat to seal on all sides. Remove from the pressure cooker. Put the trivet into the pressure cooker and add boiling, salted water up to trivet level. Place meat on trivet and season. Cook at H pressure for one hour.

Meanwhile, prepare the brown gravy, using red wine to replace some of the liquid if so desired.

When meat is cooked, put on a serving dish. (Retain the juice for future use.) Serve with rice, gravy and choice of vegetables.

Note: You can use a larger joint in this case because it is more economical. What remains can easily be reheated and eaten another day.
Serves 6.

Total time: 1 hr.

PICKLED SILVERSIDE

	Metric	Imperial	American
Water	600 ml	1 pt	2½ cups
Vinegar	300 ml	½ pt	1¼ cups
Onion, peeled and sliced	1	1	1
Mixed spices	1 tbsp	1 tbsp	1 tbsp
Salt			
Silverside	900 g	2 lb	2 lb
Flour or cornflour	1 tbsp	1 tbsp	1 tbsp

Pickling

Put the water and vinegar into a saucepan and add the onion slices, mixed spices and salt. Bring to the boil and simmer for a few minutes. Trim off any traces of fat from the meat and place in a deep casserole. Pour the hot pickling liquid over the meat and cover. Keep in a cool place for 6 days, turning the meat daily.

Cooking

Pour the pickling liquid through a sieve into a pressure cooker. Add the meat and cook for 50 minutes at H pressure. Remove the meat and keep hot. Pour a little of the pickling liquid into a small saucepan, add the flour or cornflour and blend to a smooth consistency. Gradually add the rest of the liquid, simmer and continue to stir until the gravy has thickened and cleared.

Carve the meat into slices and cover with gravy. Serve with baked potatoes and red cabbage (Page 112) or other vegetables.

Note: Serves 6.

Total time: 6 days pickling, 1 hr cooking.

CURRIED BEEF

	Metric	Imperial	American
Blade steak (preferably eye of blade)	700 g	1½ lb	1½ lb
Salt			
Stick of celery, chopped	1	1	1
Carrots, peeled and sliced	4	4	4
Large onions, peeled and sliced	2	2	2
Cooking apple, peeled and sliced	1	1	1
Sultanas	175 g	6 oz	⅔ cup
Flour	1 tbsp	1 tbsp	1 tbsp
Curry powder	1½ tbsp	1½ tbsp	1½ tbsp
Brown sugar	1 tbsp	1 tbsp	1 tbsp
Vinegar	½ tsp	½ tsp	½ tsp

Trim off all the fat from the steak then cut into small chunks. Season the meat with salt, and put on the trivet in a pressure cooker. Add salted water to trivet level. Cook for 45 minutes at H pressure.

While the meat is cooking, cook the celery, carrots and onions in salted water until tender. Add the apple and the sultanas. Bring to the boil for another minute or two, then drain, keeping the cooking liquid, and put the vegetables into a casserole.

In another saucepan blend the flour, curry powder, salt, sugar and vinegar to a smooth paste, slowly adding enough of the vegetable liquid to get the desired consistency. Simmer gently, stirring, until the mixture thickens.

MINCE LOAF WITH JACKET POTATOES

	Metric	Imperial	American
Salt and pepper			
Lean stewing steak, finely minced	700 g	1½ lb	1½ lb
Onion, peeled and chopped	1	1	1
Freshly chopped parsley, marjoram and thyme			
Milk or water	150 ml	¼ pt	⅔ cup
Breadcrumbs	1 tbsp	1 tbsp	1 tbsp
Large potatoes, washed	6	6	6

Season the minced steak and put into a large mixing bowl with the onion, parsley, marjoram and thyme. Add milk or water and mix well. Form into a loaf and cover with breadcrumbs.

Put six tablespoons of water into a roasting pan containing a trivet or wire tray. Place the meat loaf on top, cover with a layer of kitchen foil and roast in the oven for 1 hour at 400°F/200°C/ Gas mark 6. Put the potatoes in the oven at the same time, on a high shelf.

Put the cooked meat loaf into a serving dish and surround with the jacket potatoes. (Retain the juice of the roasting pan for future use.)

Note: A tasty cold dish if sliced thinly.

Total time: 1¼ hrs.

DRESSED MEAT BALLS

	Metric	Imperial	American
Minced beef or veal	700 g	1½ lb	1½ lb
Onion, peeled and finely chopped	½	½	½
Rind and juice of lemon	½	½	½
Salt and pepper			
Freshly chopped parsley and coriander			
Clove garlic, peeled and crushed	1	1	1
Cabbage	½	½	½

Put minced beef or veal, onion, lemon rind and juice, salt and pepper, parsley and coriander and garlic into a large mixing bowl and mix thoroughly. Form into eight equal, slightly flattened balls.

Separate the cabbage leaves and blanch by pouring boiling water on top. Wrap the meat balls in the cabbage leaves, and place on the trivet in a pressure cooker. Add water to trivet level. Steam at H pressure for about 10 minutes and serve on a preheated serving dish with mashed potatoes.

Total time: 20 mins.

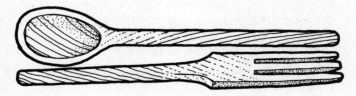

HARE AND CHICKEN PÂTÉ

	Metric	Imperial	American
Jointed hare (or 4 portions)	½	½	½
Chicken joint	1	1	1
Salt and pepper			
Onion, peeled	½	½	½
Parsley	1 sprig	1 sprig	1 sprig
Slice of brown bread	1	1	1
Port (optional)	2 tbsp	2 tbsp	2 tbsp
Yoghurt	300 ml	½ pt	1¼ cups
Bay leaf	1	1	1

Place the hare and chicken joints on the trivet in a pressure cooker, season with salt and pepper, and add salted water to trivet level. Cook for 25 minutes at H pressure.

Skin and bone the cooked joints. Put the meat, the onion and parsley through a mincer and finish with the slice of brown bread. Add port if so desired.

Place the mixture into a casserole, add the yoghurt, season and mix well. Place a bay leaf on top. Cover the casserole, put into a *bain-marie* and cook in the oven at 400°F/200°C/Gas mark 6 for 45 minutes.

Serve hot as a main course with baked potatoes and vegetables, or cold as a starter with fresh toast.

Total time: 1½ hrs.

JUGGED HARE

	Metric	Imperial	American
Hare joints	6	6	6
Stock	750 ml	1½ pt	3 cups
Red wine (optional)	250 ml	½ pt	1¼ cups
Small onion, peeled and chopped	1	1	1
Clove garlic, peeled and chopped	1	1	1
Juniper berries	1 tsp	1 tsp	1 tsp
Juice of lemon	½	½	½
Salt and pepper			
Cornflour	½ tbsp	½ tbsp	½ tbsp
Yoghurt	2 tbsp	2 tbsp	2 tbsp

Put the hare joints and the stock into a casserole. Add the onion, garlic, juniper berries and lemon juice or wine. Season with salt and pepper, cover, and put casserole into the preheated 400°F/200°C/ Gas mark 6 oven.

After 2½ hours, drain off some of the liquid into a saucepan. Add the cornflour, blend well and simmer, stirring all the time, until the sauce begins to thicken. Add the remaining liquid, blend well and add the yoghurt.

Pour the sauce over the joints, and return the casserole to the oven for a few minutes to reheat. Serve hot with noodles and red cabbage, or red-currant jelly.

Total time: 3 hrs.

RABBIT CASSEROLE

	Metric	Imperial	American
Jointed rabbit portions	6	6	6
Clove garlic, peeled	1	1	1
Small onion, peeled	1	1	1
Small carrot, peeled	1	1	1
Juice of lemon	1/2	1/2	1/2
Salt and pepper			
Stock	600 ml	1 pt	2 1/2 cups
Nutmeg	1 pinch	1 pinch	1 pinch
Thyme	1 pinch	1 pinch	1 pinch
Bay leaf	1	1	1
Cornflour	1/2 tbsp	1/2 tbsp	1/2 tbsp
Yoghurt	1 tbsp	1 tbsp	1 tbsp

Put all ingredients, except the cornflour and the yoghurt, into a casserole. Place in a preheated oven at 450°F/230°C/Gas mark 8 and cook for about 1½ hours.

Then drain a little of the liquid into a saucepan, add the cornflour and blend to a smooth paste. Add the remaining liquid, place over a gentle heat, and simmer, stirring all the time, until it thickens.

Remove the vegetables from the casserole and discard. Cover the joints with the sauce. Reheat for a few minutes in the oven. Stir in the yoghurt just before serving.

Serve hot with macaroni or brown rice, and vegetables in season.

Total time: 1 hr 50 mins.

SHRIMP CASSEROLE*

	Metric	Imperial	American
Medium size potatoes	5	5	5
Celery heart	1	1	1
Cheese sauce (Page 20)	600 ml	1 pt	2½ cups
Salt and pepper			
Shrimps, cooked and peeled	350 g	12 oz	¾ lb
Freshly chopped parsley			

Cook the potatoes in salted water until tender but still firm. Cook the celery in the same way (or use canned celery if you prefer).

Prepare the cheese sauce, and keep warm.

Peel the potatoes, slice and cover the bottom of the casserole with half the slices. Season with salt and pepper. Add a layer of celery slices and a layer of shrimps. Top with the remaining potato slices. Cover with the cheese sauce, then put into the preheated 400°F/200°C/Gas mark 6 oven for 20 minutes.

Sprinkle with a little fresh chopped parsley before serving hot with a salad.

Note: Instead of shrimps, cooked skinned diced chicken can be used.

Total time: 45 mins.

VENISON STEAKS

	Metric	Imperial	American
Cumberland sauce (Page 23)			
Venison steak (per person)	1	1	1
Salt and pepper			

Make the Cumberland sauce and put into a sauce boat.

Season each steak with salt and pepper. Put three tablespoons of water into a frying pan, heat gently, add the steaks and cook for a few minutes over a medium heat. Then turn and cook the other side in the same way, until tender. Put the steaks on a preheated serving dish and serve hot with potatoes and the Cumberland sauce.

Total time: 25 mins.

STEWED VENISON

	Metric	Imperial	American
Venison	700 g	1½ lb	1½ lb
Juniper berries or mixed spices	1 tsp	1 tsp	1 tsp
Bay leaf	1	1	1
Salt and pepper			
Juice of lemon	½	½	½
Cornflour	2 tsp	2 tsp	2 tsp

Remove any skin from the venison and chop the meat into small chunks. Put salted water to trivet level in a pressure cooker. Add juniper berries or mixed spices and the bay leaf. Season the meat with salt and pepper and sprinkle with lemon juice. Cook for 45 minutes at H pressure. Put the cooked meat into a casserole and keep hot.

Put the cornflour into a saucepan, add a little of the strained venison juices from the pressure cooker and blend to a smooth paste. Slowly add the rest of the venison juices and simmer, stirring all the time, until it thickens and clears. Pour the sauce over the meat in the casserole, cover and put into the oven to heat through.

Serve hot with red cabbage (Page 112) and potatoes.

Total time: 45 mins.

SPAGHETTI WITH CHICKEN LIVERS*

	Metric	Imperial	American
Spaghetti	350 g	12 oz	¾ lb
Chicken or turkey liver	350 g	12 oz	¾ lb
Small onion, peeled and sliced	½	½	½
Salt and pepper			
Tomato sauce (Page 19)	600 ml	1 pt	2½ cups

Cook the spaghetti in plenty of salted water as directed on the packet.

Put two tablespoons of water into a frying pan and add the liver and the onion. Cover and simmer gently for about 10 minutes, taking care not to let it get dry. Season with salt and pepper.

Meanwhile, prepare the tomato sauce.

When the spaghetti is ready, drain well. Arrange the spaghetti in a circle on an ovenproof dish and heap the cooked liver and onion in the centre. Add the tomato sauce, pouring it over the spaghetti only and serve hot.

Note: This makes an easy and very reasonably priced main course which is unusual and attractive in looks and taste.

Total time: 35 mins.

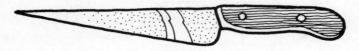

LIVER CASSEROLE*

	Metric	Imperial	American
Liver, chopped	350 g	12 oz	¾ lb
Potatoes, peeled and sliced	4	4	4
Onions, peeled and sliced	2	2	2
Carrots, peeled and sliced	2	2	2
Stock	375 ml	¾ pt	2 cups
Salt and pepper			
Mixed herbs	1 tsp	1 tsp	1 tsp
Bay leaf	1	1	1

Place the liver, potatoes, onions and carrots in a casserole in alternate layers, finishing with a layer of potato.

Season the stock with salt, pepper and herbs and pour it over the layers in the casserole. Place the bay leaf on top, cover and cook in a preheated 450°F/230°C/Gas mark 8 oven for 25 minutes.

After 25 minutes remove the lid and the bay leaf, and cook for another 10 minutes to give the potatoes a golden crust. Serve immediately.

Total time: 45 mins.

CURRIED RICE WITH CHICKEN LIVERS*

	Metric	Imperial	American
Long grain rice	250 g	9 oz	1½ cups
Carrots, peeled and diced	3	3	3
Peas, shelled	175 g	6 oz	⅔ cup
Chicken livers, fresh or frozen	450 g	1 lb	1 lb
Small onion, peeled and cut into rings	1	1	1
Curry powder	1 tbsp	1 tbsp	1 tbsp
Salt			

Put the rice into a saucepan, add three times the volume of boiling salted water and simmer until the water is absorbed.

Meanwhile, cook the carrots with the peas in salted water until tender.

Halve the chicken livers and put them with the onion rings into a frying pan, with three table-spoons of water. Cover and simmer for about 5 minutes.

Drain the rice and the vegetables and put into a warmed casserole. Add the curry powder and mix well. Make a hollow in the middle of the mixture. Season the liver and onion with salt and place in the hollow. Cover and put into the pre-heated oven to heat through. Serve hot. Chutney makes a good accompaniment.

Total time: 40 mins.

LASAGNE*

	Metric	Imperial	American
Lasagne	225 g	8 oz	½ lb
Mushrooms, washed and chopped	100 g	4 oz	¼ lb
Chicken livers, chopped	350 g	12 oz	¾ lb
Small onion, peeled and sliced	1	1	1
Cheese sauce (Page 20)	750 ml	1¼ pt	3 cups
Salt			
Tomatoes, sliced	350 g	12 oz	¾ lb

Cook the lasagne following the instructions on the packet. Stir well to prevent sticking. Drain off the liquid.

Meanwhile, put two tablespoons of water into a frying pan, add the mushrooms, liver and onion, cover and cook for 10 minutes, taking care not to let it boil dry and stirring from time to time.

Prepare the cheese sauce.

Put a layer of lasagne into a deep casserole. Cover with part of the chicken liver mix and sprinkle with salt. Pour a layer of the cheese sauce on top. Add a second layer of lasagne and top with tomatoes. Sprinkle with salt and pour another layer of the cheese sauce on top. Add a third layer of lasagne, and cover with a second layer of chicken liver mix and cheese sauce. Continue with alternate layers until all the ingredients are used up, keeping enough cheese sauce to cover the top. Put the casserole into the preheated 400°F/200°C/Gas mark 6 oven to heat through for 20 minutes.

Serve with salad, and follow with a light sweet, since this is quite a filling dish.

Total time: 1 hr 20 mins.

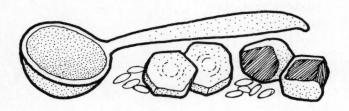

LIVER AND ONION*

	Metric	Imperial	American
Water OR	3 tbsp	3 tbsp	3 tbsp
white wine (optional)	3 tbsp	3 tbsp	3 tbsp
Small onion, peeled and cut into rings	1	1	1
Slices of liver	4	4	4
Salt and pepper			
Freshly chopped parsley, tarragon and chervil			

Put the water or wine into a frying pan and add the onion rings and the liver. Cover and simmer for a few minutes, then turn and simmer again until the liver is cooked through. Season with salt and pepper and add herbs. Place on a warmed serving dish and serve immediately. A purée of spinach goes well with this dish.

Total time: 20 mins.

MIXED PANCAKES

	Metric	Imperial	American
Double the amount of basic pancake batter (Page 44)			
Spinach	450 g	1 lb	1 lb
Salt and pepper			
Mushrooms, washed and sliced	225 g	8 oz	½ lb
Large tomato, sliced	1	1	1
Cottage cheese or skimmed milk soft cheese	225 g	8 oz	½ lb

Make basic pancakes. Cook spinach and season with salt and pepper. Drain well and liquidize. Keep hot.

Season the mushrooms with salt and pepper and cook in a frying pan with two tablespoons of water for 3 minutes. Keep hot.

Season the tomato with salt, and add a little salt to the cheese. Fill the pancakes with alternate layers of spinach, tomato, mushrooms and cheese. Roll each pancake up and put in an oven-proof dish. Place in 350°F/180°C/Gas mark 4 oven to reheat for 15 minutes.

Note: These pancakes make a pleasant change from more traditional main courses.

Total time: 1 hr.

FILLED GREEN PEPPERS

	Metric	Imperial	American
Cooked chicken joints, skinned and boned	2	2	2
Onion, peeled	1/2	1/2	1/2
Mushrooms, washed	100 g	4 oz	1/4 lb
Salt and pepper			
Mixed herbs	1 pinch	1 pinch	1 pinch
Large green pepper (per person)	1	1	1
Egg	1	1	1
Yoghurt	4 tbsp	4 tbsp	4 tbsp
French mustard	1/2 tsp	1/2 tsp	1/2 tsp

Mince the chicken meat together with the onion and mushrooms, add salt, pepper and herbs and mix well.

Carefully cut off the tops of the green peppers and remove pith and pips. Blanch in a saucepan of salted boiling water, simmering for a few minutes. Place in an ovenproof dish.

Fill the peppers with the chicken mixture, and cover with the tops. Put into a preheated 375°F/190°C/Gas mark 5 oven and cook for 40 minutes.

Meanwhile, whisk the egg, yoghurt and mustard together. Pour into the cooked peppers, and return to the oven for another 10 minutes to set the topping. Serve hot with baked potatoes and a mixed salad.

Total time: 1 hr.

FONDUE CHINOISE*

	Metric	Imperial	American
Small potatoes	450 g	1 lb	1 lb
Veal escalopes	225 g	8 oz	½ lb
Calves liver	225 g	8 oz	½ lb
Button mushrooms, washed and quartered	225 g	8 oz	½ lb
Tomatoes, quartered	3	3	3
Can of asparagus tips, drained	1	1	1
Cranberry jelly			
Pickled onions			
Gherkins			
Tangerine sections			
Green peppers, de-seeded and sliced			
Salt and pepper			
Meat stock (Page 14)	750 ml	1¼ pt	3 cups

Cook the potatoes in boiling salted water, drain well, put in a covered casserole and keep hot.

Cut the veal and the liver into thin slivers and arrange neatly on a flat dish.

Put all the ingredients, except the stock and meat, into separate small bowls and dishes. Place the fondue dish in the centre of the table and arrange the bowls and dishes around it.

Just before sitting down to eat, fill the fondue dish with very hot, but not quite boiling, lean meat stock. Light the flame under it and bring to the boil. Put the warm potatoes on the table.

COLD BUFFETS

VEAL IN ASPIC

	Metric	Imperial	American
Lean veal	700 g	1½ lb	1½ lb
Salt and pepper			
Bay leaf	1	1	1
Aspic powder	1 pkt	1 pkt	1 pkt
Juice of lemon	1	1	1
Worcestershire sauce	5 drops	5 drops	5 drops

Put salted water to trivet level in a pressure cooker. Remove all fat from the veal then cut into cubes. Season with salt and pepper and place on the trivet in the pressure cooker with the bay leaf on top. Cook at H pressure for 30 minutes.

When cooked, remove the meat and cool the meat stock quickly. When the stock is cold, remove all fat from the top.

Dissolve the aspic as directed on the packet, using reheated meat stock. Pour the aspic into a deep serving dish, add the cooked veal cubes, lemon juice and Worcestershire sauce and leave to set. Serve chilled with mixed salad and new potatoes.

Total time: 40 mins.

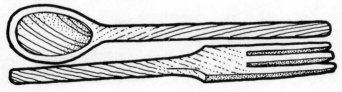

HADDOCK IN ASPIC

	Metric	Imperial	American
Haddock fillets, skinned	700 g	1½ lb	1½ lb
Juice of lemon	1	1	1
Salt and pepper			
Aspic powder	1 pkt	1 pkt	1 pkt
Green or red pepper, de-seeded and finely sliced	1	1	1
Cucumber, cubed	¼	¼	¼

Put the haddock in a frying pan or shallow sauce-pan and add a little water, lemon juice, salt and pepper. Cover and simmer until tender. Strain, keeping the liquid.

Dissolve aspic as directed on the packet, using the hot liquid. When dissolved, make up the required quantity with remaining liquid or water.

Cut the fillets into small portions and put into the dissolved aspic. Add pepper and cucumber to the haddock fillets in the aspic. Leave to cool and set. Serve with lettuce or tomato salad.

Note: Cod fillets can be used instead of haddock.

Total time: 30 mins + setting time.

CHICKEN IN ASPIC

	Metric	Imperial	American
Chicken joints	3	3	3
Aspic powder	1 pkt	1 pkt	1 pkt
Chicken stock or water	600 ml	1 pt	2½ cups
Marmite (if water is used)	½ tbsp	½ tbsp	½ tbsp
Juice of lemon	½	½	½
Salt			
Worcestershire sauce	3 drops	3 drops	3 drops
Carrots, peeled	225 g	8 oz	½ lb
Green peas	225 g	8 oz	½ lb
Freshly chopped parsley			

Place chicken joints in a pressure cooker on the trivet. Add salted water to level of trivet and cook at H pressure for 20 minutes.

Meanwhile, dissolve aspic as directed on packet, using either hot chicken stock or water. Add the remainder of the liquid. If water is used, stir in the Marmite. Add the lemon juice, salt and Worcestershire sauce. Leave to cool.

Skin and bone the chicken joints and chop into small pieces. Cook carrots and peas in salted water until tender. Drain. Dice the cooked carrots.

Put the chicken, carrots and peas into the cooled aspic, sprinkle with chopped parsley and mix well. Leave to cool and then set in fridge.

Serve as a main meal on a hot summer day, or as a starter (reducing the quantities).

Total time: 40 mins + setting time.

TURKEY SALAD

	Metric	Imperial	American
Lettuce, washed and drained	1	1	1
Cooked turkey joints, skinned, boned and sliced	4	4	4
Small can of pineapple chunks	1	1	1
Cucumber, sliced	½	½	½
Tomatoes, quartered	4	4	4
Pink salad dressing (Page 120)	600 ml	1 pt	2½ cups

Line a serving dish with lettuce leaves. Arrange the meat in the centre of the lettuce leaves and surround it with the pineapple, cucumber and tomatoes. Chill.

Make the pink salad dressing. Serve cold with the dressing and hot new potatoes.

Total time: 10 mins.

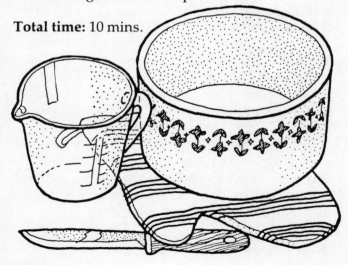

RICE SALAD

	Metric	Imperial	American
Long grain rice	350 g	12 oz	1½ cups
Chicken joints OR	2	2	2
Fish	450 g	1 lb	1 lb
Peas OR	100 g	4 oz	¼ lb
Cucumber	½	½	½
Tomatoes	2	2	2
Pink salad dressing (Page 120)	600 ml	1 pt	2½ cups

Cook the rice in three times its own volume of salted water until tender, then drain.

Cook the chicken joints or the fish, remove skin and bones and cut flesh into small portions. Cook the peas in salted water until tender, then cool, or cut the cucumber into small cubes. Cut the tomatoes into cubes.

Put all ingredients, except the dressing, into a serving dish, mix well and chill.

Make the pink salad dressing and serve chilled with the rice salad.

Note: You might find it practical to use this recipe with leftover fish, chicken or shrimps.*

Total time: 30 mins + cooling time.

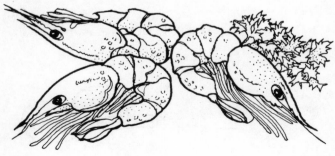

VEGETABLES & VEGETABLE DISHES

LEEKS IN WHITE SAUCE

	Metric	Imperial	American
Leeks, washed	4	4	4
Basic white sauce (Page 16)	375 ml	¾ pt	2 cups
Juice of lemon	½	½	½
Freshly chopped parsley			

Cook the leeks in salted water until tender.

Meanwhile prepare the white sauce, and keep hot.

Drain the cooked leeks and put into a vegetable dish. Quickly stir the lemon juice into the white sauce and pour over the leeks. Garnish with parsley.

Serve hot with meat, or increase the quantities and serve with baked potatoes as a main course.

Total time: 30 mins.

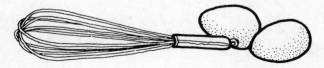

CAULIFLOWER CHEESE

	Metric	Imperial	American
Large cauliflower	1	1	1
Salt			
Cheese sauce (Page 20)	375 ml	¾ pt	2 cups

Remove the outer leaves from the cauliflower and carefully trim away most of the stalk, leaving a flat base. Put into salted water in a deep saucepan, bring to the boil, then lower the heat and simmer for about 15 minutes (depending on size) until tender, but not soft or broken.

Meanwhile, make the cheese sauce.

Drain the cauliflower, put into an ovenproof dish and pour the cheese sauce on top. Put into a preheated oven and brown for about 10 minutes.

Serve with baked potatoes or freshly made toast. This makes a good main course after a pâté starter.

Total time: 30 mins.

RED CABBAGE SPECIAL

	Metric	Imperial	American
Red cabbage, finely grated	1	1	1
Cooking apple, cored and grated	1	1	1
Water	150 ml	¼ pt	⅓ cup
Vinegar	4 tbs	4 tbs	4 tbs
Sultanas	2 tbsp	2 tbsp	2 tbsp
Salt			
Brown sugar	1 tbsp	1 tbsp	1 tbsp

Put cabbage into a colander and pour boiling water on top. Leave to drain.

Put cabbage, apple, water, vinegar, sultanas, salt and brown sugar into a pressure cooker and cook for 20 minutes at H pressure. Then drain off surplus liquid. Taste, and if necessary add vinegar and/or sugar and salt to sharpen the flavour.

Serve hot in a casserole with stew or pot roast.

Total time: 30 mins.

RATATOUILLE

	Metric	Imperial	American
Onion, peeled and sliced	1	1	1
Tomatoes, peeled and chopped	225 g	8 oz	½ lb
Courgettes, sliced	225 g	8 oz	½ lb
Tomato purée	2 tbsp	2 tbsp	2 tbsp
Salt and pepper			

Put the onion, tomatoes, courgettes and tomato purée into a saucepan. Add just enough water to prevent burning. Season to taste, cover, bring to the boil, and simmer for 15 minutes, stirring occasionally.

When cooked, remove any excess liquid, and save for soup or stock. Serve hot with a joint of meat or with boiled potatoes or pasta.

Note: This dish can be varied by using peppers or aubergines (egg plant) instead of courgettes.

Total time: 30 mins.

MASHED POTATOES

	Metric	Imperial	American
Potatoes, peeled and halved	900 g	2 lb	2 lb
Milk	300 ml	½ pt	1¼ cups
Salt			
Freshly chopped parsley			

Cook the potatoes until tender in a saucepan or for 10 minutes in a pressure cooker.

Drain off the water and put the potatoes into a mixing bowl. Add milk and salt to taste, and whisk until the potatoes are fluffy. Serve sprinkled with a little parsley.

Total time: 15 mins.

COURGETTES

	Metric	Imperial	American
Courgettes	450 g	1 lb	1 lb
Salt and pepper			

Slice the courgettes into ½ inch (1 cm) rings, and put into a saucepan. Season with salt and pepper to taste, and simmer with very little water for a few minutes until tender. Serve hot with any meat.

Total time: 15 mins.

COURGETTES À LA TOMATE

	Metric	Imperial	American
Courgettes, sliced in rings	450 g	1 lb	1 lb
Small onion, peeled and sliced	1	1	1
Tomatoes, quartered	225 g	8 oz	½ lb
Salt and pepper			
Freshly chopped dill			

Put the courgettes, onion and tomatoes and dill into a frying pan or saucepan, season with salt and pepper to taste and add just enough water to prevent sticking. Cook for about 15 minutes, or until tender. Garnish with dill. Serve hot with any meat.

Total time: 25 mins.

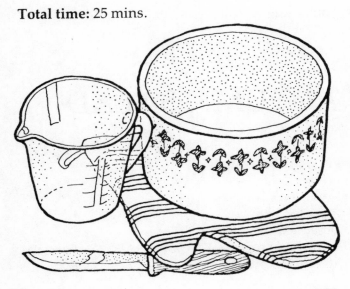

SALADS

CHICORY SALAD

	Metric	Imperial	American
Grapefruit	2	2	2
Heads of chicory	2	2	2

Peel the grapefruit and cut into small chunks. Put into a salad bowl. Slice the chicory, starting at the top and discarding the bottom since it tends to be bitter. Add the sliced chicory to the grapefruit and mix well. Serve without any dressing.

Note: This salad goes well with cold meats and is very refreshing.

Total time: 10 mins.

AUTUMN SALAD

	Metric	Imperial	American
Pink salad dressing (Page 120)			
Very small onion, peeled	1	1	1
Dessert apples, washed and cored	450 g	1 lb	1 lb
Juice of lemon	1	1	1

116

Prepare the pink salad dressing.

Grate the onion and apples and sprinkle with lemon juice. Pour the pink salad dressing on top, mix well and serve immediately.

This salad is excellent with chicken or liver pâté, or any cold meat.

Note: Apples tend to discolour, so prepare the salad shortly before serving.

Total time: 15 mins.

MUSHROOM SALAD

	Metric	Imperial	American
Curd or cottage cheese	225 g	8 oz	½ lb
Juice of lemon	½	½	½
Salt and pepper			
Freshly chopped parsley and coriander			
Button mushrooms, washed and sliced	450 g	1 lb	1 lb

Put the cheese, lemon juice, salt and pepper and herbs into a salad bowl. Whip with a whisk or fork to a creamy consistency. (If too thick, add a little milk.) Add the mushrooms and mix gently.

Serve cold as a starter or as a salad with fish or meat.

Total time: 10 mins.

CHINESE SALAD

	Metric	Imperial	American
Pink salad dressing (Page 120)	300 ml	½ pt	1¼ cups
Cottage cheese	225 g	8 oz	½ lb
Salt			
Tomato, thinly sliced	1	1	1
Grapefruit, peeled	½	½	½
Chinese cabbage, shredded	½	½	½

Prepare pink salad dressing.

Season the cottage cheese with salt and mix well. Place in the centre of a large salad bowl. Decorate the cheese with tomato slices.

Divide the grapefruit into segments. Pile the cabbage around the cheese. Top with the grapefruit segments and serve chilled with the pink salad dressing.

Total time: 15 mins.

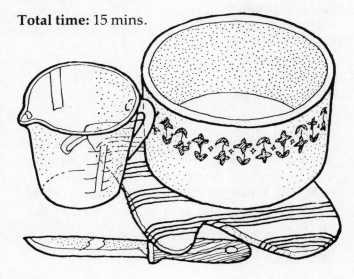

GREEN PEPPER SALAD

	Metric	Imperial	American
Curd or cottage cheese	225 g	8 oz	½lb
Yoghurt	½ tbsp	½ tbsp	½ tbsp
Salt			
Caraway seeds	½ tsp	½ tsp	½ tsp
Sweet paprika	1 tsp	1 tsp	1 tsp
Capers, chopped	4	4	4
Slices of onion, chopped	2	2	2
Cos lettuce, shredded	1	1	1
Green pepper, de-seeded and thinly sliced	1	1	1

Put the cheese and the yoghurt into the mixing bowl and season with salt to taste. Add the caraway seeds, paprika, capers and onion and mix well.

Place the cheese mixture in the centre of a salad bowl and surround with shredded lettuce and the sliced pepper. Serve chilled.

This makes a good summer lunch, served with brown toast.

Total time: 15 mins.

SALAD DRESSINGS

GREEN SALAD DRESSING

	Metric	Imperial	American
Cooked spinach	1 tbsp	1 tbsp	1 tbsp
Yoghurt	150 ml	¼ pt	⅔ cup
Juice of lemon	½	½	½
Sugar	1 tsp	1 tsp	1 tsp
Salt and pepper			

Put the spinach, yoghurt, lemon juice, sugar, salt and pepper into a blender and liquidize. Chill. Serve in a jug or sauceboat, with salads needing a colour contrast.

Total time: 10 mins.

PINK SALAD DRESSING

	Metric	Imperial	American
Yoghurt	300 ml	½ pt	1¼ cups
Tomato purée	½ tbsp	½ tbsp	½ tbsp
Caster sugar	1 tsp	1 tsp	1 tsp
Juice of lemon	½	½	½
Salt			
French mustard	1 tsp	1 tsp	1 tsp

Put the yoghurt into a mixing bowl, add the tomato purée, sugar, lemon juice, salt and French mustard and blend to a creamy consistency. Serve chilled.

Note: This salad dressing will keep for up to four days in the refrigerator, if put into an airtight container.

Total time: 10 mins.

WHITE SALAD DRESSING

	Metric	Imperial	American
Egg white	1	1	1
Yoghurt	150 ml	¼ pt	⅔ cup
Vinegar	1 tsp	1 tsp	1 tsp
Freshly chopped parsley, chives or dill			
Salt and pepper			

Beat the egg white until stiff. Carefully fold in the yoghurt, the vinegar and the herbs. Season with salt and pepper. Serve with salads.

Note: This dressing will not keep so prepare it just before it is needed.

Total time: 10 mins.

CHEESE WHIPS

PLAIN WHIP

	Metric	Imperial	American
Curd or cottage cheese	225 g	8 oz	½ lb
Salt			
Yoghurt (if curd cheese is used)	½ tbsp	½ tbsp	½ tbsp

Whisk the cheese and a pinch of salt together to form a smooth cream. If curd cheese is used, thin with a dessertspoon of yoghurt. Put into a butter dish or bowl and serve chilled.

This whip may be used instead of butter on toast. It should be mild enough for spreading with jam or marmalade instead of butter.

Total time: 5 mins.

GARLIC WHIP

	Metric	Imperial	American
Clove, garlic	1	1	1
Salt			
Cottage or curd cheese	225 g	8 oz	½ lb
Yoghurt (if curd cheese is used)	½ tbsp	½ tbsp	½ tbsp

Crush the garlic on a chopping board with a little salt. Put cheese, garlic, and salt to taste into a mixing bowl and whisk to a creamy consistency. (Thin with yoghurt if curd cheese is used.) Put into a butter dish or small bowl.

Serve chilled. This is an ideal whip for parties, or as a spread.

Total time: 5 mins.

PAPRIKA WHIP

	Metric	Imperial	American
Cottage or curd cheese	225 g	8 oz	½ lb
Yoghurt (if curd cheese is used)	½ tbsp	½ tbsp	½ tbsp
Sweet paprika	1 tsp	1 tsp	1 tsp
Capers, finely chopped	6	6	6
Caraway seeds	½ tsp	½ tsp	½ tsp
Small onion, peeled and finely chopped	½	½	½
Salt			
Parsley	1 sprig	1 sprig	1 sprig

Put the cottage cheese (or curd cheese and yoghurt) into a mixing bowl. Add the paprika, capers, caraway seeds, onion and salt and whisk to a smooth cream. Put into a butter dish or bowl, and decorate with a sprig of parsley.

Serve chilled. Ideal as a spread or dip.

Total time: 5 mins.

CHIVE WHIP

	Metric	Imperial	American
Cottage or curd cheese	225 g	8 oz	½ lb
Freshly chopped chives	1 tsp	1 tsp	1 tsp
Yoghurt (if curd cheese is used)	½ tbsp	½ tbsp	½ tbsp
Salt			

Whisk the cheese, chives and salt together to form a smooth cream. If curd cheese is used, thin with a little yoghurt. Put into a butter dish or small bowl.

Serve chilled. This is an ideal dip for parties, as well as being a delicious spread.

Total time: 5 mins.

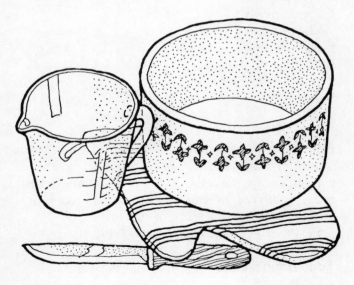

CUCUMBER WHIP

	Metric	Imperial	American
Cottage cheese	225 g	8 oz	½ lb
Cucumber, cubed	½	½	½
Spring onion, peeled and finely chopped	1	1	1
Freshly chopped dill or parsley			
Salt			

Put the cottage cheese into a mixing bowl. Add the cucumber, onion and herbs, season to taste and mix well. Turn out into a bowl and chill.

Serve as spread on toast or fresh bread, or as a dip for parties.

Total time: 5 mins.

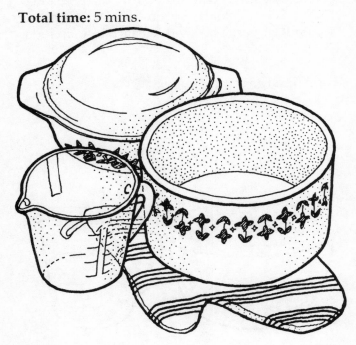

DESSERTS

BAKED APPLES

	Metric	Imperial	American
Cooking apple (per person) washed and cored	1	1	1
Honey (per apple)	1 tsp	1 tsp	1 tsp
Sultanas (per apple)	1 tsp	1 tsp	1 tsp

Make a thin, skin-deep cut horizontally right round each apple. Fill each apple with honey and sultanas. Sprinkle with water. Put into preheated 375°F/190°C/Gas mark 5 oven and bake for about 30 minutes. Serve hot with custard in individual bowls.

Total time: 35 mins.

SWEET PANCAKES

	Metric	Imperial	American
Basic pancake batter (Page 44)			
Jam, marmalade, honey or lemon juice	*4 tbsp*	*4 tbsp*	*4 tbsp*

Make the basic pancakes and spread each pancake thinly with whichever filling is preferred. Roll up and keep hot in an ovenproof dish.

The basic pancake quantities should make six pancakes. Increase or decrease the quantity according to the type of meal you are serving.

Total time: 30 mins.

CHRISTMAS PUDDING

	Metric	Imperial	American
Self-raising flour	2 tsp	2 tsp	2 tsp
Brown sugar	2 tsp	2 tsp	2 tsp
Fresh breadcrumbs	2 tbsp	2 tbsp	2 tbsp
Mixed spices	½ tsp	½ tsp	½ tsp
Sultanas	350 g	12 oz	2 cups
Prunes, stoned and chopped	100 g	4 oz	¼ lb
Mixed peel	½ tbsp	½ tbsp	½ tbsp
Juice and finely grated rind of lemon	½	½	½
Honey	1 tbsp	1 tbsp	1 tbsp
Marmalade	2 tbsp	2 tbsp	2 tbsp
Milk OR	150 ml	¼ pt	⅔ cup
Brandy	150 ml	¼ pt	⅔ cup

Put all the dry ingredients into a mixing bowl and mix well. Add all the remaining ingredients *except* the milk or brandy and mix well. Add enough milk or brandy to form a stiff dough. Turn into a pudding basin, and cover tightly with kitchen foil. Steam in a pressure cooker for 1½ hours, or in a *bain-marie* for 3 hours.

Note: Prepare this pudding only two or three days before Christmas as it will not keep as long as the normal Christmas pudding. Serve with custard instead of brandy butter.

Total time: 1 hr 40 mins.

MERINGUES

	Metric	Imperial	American
Egg whites	4	4	4
Caster sugar	225 g	8 oz	1 cup

Whisk the egg whites until stiff, then carefully fold in the sugar. Line a baking tray with grease-proof paper and drop dessertspoons of the mix on to it. Bake in the preheated 250°F/130°C/Gas mark ½ oven for 3 hours. Serve with any stewed fruit or fruit salad.

Total time: 3 hrs.

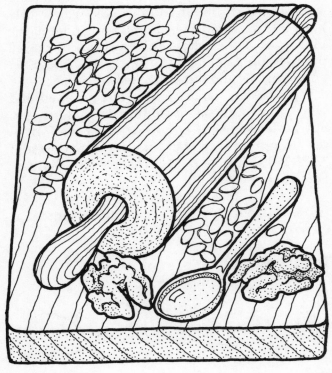

PINEAPPLE MERINGUE

	Metric	Imperial	American
Cornflour	½ tbsp	½ tbsp	½ tbsp
Can of pineapple chunks	450 g	1 lb	1 lb
Eggs	2	2	2
Granulated sugar	½ tbsp	½ tbsp	½ tbsp
Caster sugar	3 tbsp	3 tbsp	3 tbsp

Blend the cornflour with a little of the pineapple juice. Break the eggs and separate the yolks from the whites. Add one yolk and the granulated sugar to the cornflour and mix well with a fork. Pour into a saucepan. Add the remainder of the pineapple juice. Simmer on a low heat, stirring all the time until smooth and thick. Add the pineapple chunks and put into ovenproof dish.

Put the egg whites into a mixing bowl and whisk until stiff, slowly adding the caster sugar. Spread the whisked egg whites over the fruit in the ovenproof dish. Put into preheated oven at 375°F/190°C/Gas mark 5 and bake for 10 minutes. Serve hot or cold.

Note: This pudding can also be made with mandarin oranges.

Total time: 20 mins.

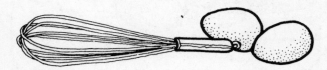

PAVLOVA

	Metric	Imperial	American
Egg whites	3	3	3
Caster sugar	175 g	6 oz	¾ cup
Vinegar	½ tsp	½ tsp	½ tsp
Cornflour	1 tsp	1 tsp	1 tsp
Raspberries or strawberries			

Put the egg whites into a mixing bowl and whisk, slowly adding half the sugar. Continue until the mixture is very stiff. Fold in the rest of the sugar, the vinegar and the cornflour. Line a baking tin with greaseproof paper and turn out the mix on to it. Place in preheated 370°F/190°C/Gas mark 5 oven and bake for 10 minutes. Then reduce the oven temperature to 250°F/130°C/Gas mark ½ and continue baking the pavlova at this temperature for 1½ hours.

Remove from the oven and leave to cool. This meringue should be white outside, with a soft centre. Serve with raspberries or strawberries.

Total time: 1¾ hrs.

FRUIT WHIP

	Metric	Imperial	American
Grapefruit, peeled OR	1	1	1
Oranges, peeled	2	2	2
Apples, washed and cored	3	3	3
Yoghurt	75 ml	⅛ pt	⅜ cup
Sugar			

Divide the oranges or the grapefruit into segments and put into a blender. Cut the apples into pieces and add to the blender with the yoghurt and sugar to taste. Liquidize. Chill in the refrigerator. Serve in a fruit bowl.

Note: Any fruit in season can be used instead of oranges or grapefruit, but then some lemon juice should always be added. Bananas give this sweet more body and a very different taste.

Total time: 10 mins.

RHUBARB WHIP

	Metric	Imperial	American
Rhubarb, washed and cubed	450 g	1 lb	1 lb
Brown sugar	4 tbsp	4 tbsp	4 tbsp
Strawberry jelly	1 pkt	1 pkt	1 pkt

Put the rhubarb into a saucepan with the sugar and a little water and cook until tender.

Dissolve the jelly as directed on the packet, using the liquid from the cooked rhubarb instead of water. Add the dissolved jelly to the rhubarb and leave it to cool. Then put into the blender and liquidize. Pour into the fruit bowl and leave to set.

Serve with meringues or decorate with fresh strawberries.

Total time: 20 mins plus setting time.

SUPER WHIP

	Metric	Imperial	American
Curd cheese	450 g	1 lb	1 lb
Yoghurt	300 ml	½ pt	1¼ cups
Sultanas, washed	1 tbsp	1 tbsp	1 tbsp
Caster sugar	200 g	7 oz	1 cup

Put all the ingredients into a bowl and whisk well but do not crush the sultanas. Turn the mixture into a serving dish, piling it high, and serve chilled.

Total time: 10 mins.

FRUIT AMBROSIA

	Metric	Imperial	America
Apples, peeled, cored and chopped	2	2	2
Orange, peeled and chopped	1	1	1
Banana, peeled and chopped	1	1	1
Sugar			
Orange or pineapple juice	1 tbsp	1 tbsp	1 tbsp

Put the apples, orange and banana and the fruit juice into a blender with sugar to taste. Liquidize and chill. Serve cold in small individual dishes.

Total time: 20 mins.

PEACH SNOW

	Metric	Imperial	American
Large can of peaches	1	1	1
Gelatine	1 pkt	1 pkt	1 pkt
Juice of lemon	½	½	½
Egg whites	2	2	2

Strain the juice from the can of peaches. Dissolve the gelatine as directed on packet, using hot fruit juice instead of water. Then make up required quantity with the remaining fruit juice. Add the lemon juice and the strained peaches and liquidize. Leave to cool.

Whisk the egg whites until stiff and add to the cooled jelly. Return the mixture to blender, liquidize again and turn into a fruit bowl. Set in the refrigerator. Serve chilled.

Note: Other fruits may be used in the same way.

Total time: 10 mins plus setting time.

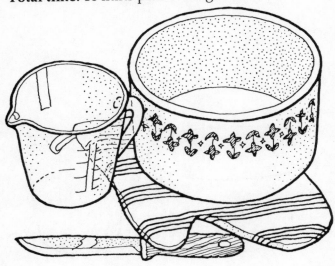

APPLE SNOW

	Metric	Imperial	American
Cooking apples, peeled and cored	450 g	1 lb	1 lb
Juice and rind of lemon	1	1	1
Sugar	50 g	2 oz	¼ cup
Yoghurt	1 tbsp	1 tbsp	1 tbsp
Egg whites	2	2	2

Cover the base of a saucepan with a little water, add the apples and lemon juice and cook gently until tender. Add the sugar and leave to cool. Then turn into blender and liquidize to a thick purée. Pour into a fruit bowl. Add the yoghurt and the grated lemon rind. Whisk the egg whites until stiff and fold in. Chill. Serve cold with small meringues.

Total time: 20 mins.

ORANGE FLUFF

	Metric	Imperial	American
Oranges	2	2	2
Water	150 ml	1/4 pt	2/3 cup
Gelatine	15 g	1/2 oz	2 tbsp
Egg whites	2	2	2
Sugar	85 g	3 oz	3/8 cup
Glacé cherries			

Peel the rind very thinly from the oranges, then squeeze out the orange juice into a mixing bowl.

Put the water into a saucepan, add the orange rind and bring slowly to the boil. Strain into a basin and dissolve the gelatine in the liquid. Leave to cool.

Put the egg whites into a mixing bowl, add the sugar and the dissolved cooled gelatine and whisk until light and fluffy.

Serve either piled into a large bowl, or in individual dishes, decorated with glacé cherries.

Total time: 20 mins.

CHESTNUT SWEET

	Metric	Imperial	American
Can of chestnut purée, unsweetened	1	1	1
Maple syrup	6 tbsp	6 tbsp	6 tbsp
Lemon juice			

Put the chestnut purée and maple syrup into a blender and liquidize. Add lemon juice to taste. Serve in individual dishes.

Total time: 10 mins.

JELLY SURPRISE

	Metric	Imperial	American
Gelatine	15 g	1/2 oz	2 tbsp
Pineapple juice	600 ml	1 pt	2 1/2 cups
Sponge cake (Page 149), sliced	4 slices	4 slices	4 slices

Dissolve the gelatine as directed on the packet, using some of the pineapple juice instead of water.

Arrange the sponge cake slices in a serving dish. Pour a little pineapple juice on each slice. Stir the remainder of the pineapple juice into the dissolved gelatine. Pour over the sponge cake. Cool and set in the refrigerator.

Total time: 10 mins plus setting time.

MORELLO JELLY

	Metric	Imperial	American
Large can of Morello cherries	1	1	1
Cornflour	½ tbsp	½ tbsp	½ tbsp
Water			

Drain the juice from the can of cherries. Add enough water to the juice to make up to one pint (500 ml, 2 cups). Put the cornflour into a saucepan and blend to a smooth paste with a little of the juice. Add the remainder of the liquid and simmer gently over a low heat, stirring all the time, until the mixture thickens. Pour into a serving dish or individual bowls, add the cherries and chill. Serve cold as a dessert.

Total time: 10 mins plus setting time.

FRUIT DUMPLINGS

	Metric	Imperial	American
Curd or cottage cheese	225 g	8 oz	½ lb
Self-raising flour	1½ tbsp	1½ tbsp	1½ tbsp
Breadcrumbs	1½ tbsp	1½ tbsp	1½ tbsp
Semolina	3 tbsp	3 tbsp	3 tbsp
Egg	1	1	1
Plums, apricots or cherries			
Water	1.4 lit	4 pts	4 pts
Salt	1 pinch	1 pinch	1 pinch

Put all the ingredients, except the fruit, salt and water, into a bowl and mix together. Turn out on to a floured board and with floured hands form into a sausage about 2 inches (5 cm) thick. Cut into ½ inch (2 cm) slices and wrap each slice round a plum, apricot or two cherries. With floured hands lightly roll each dumpling to seal the fruit in.

Put the water into a large saucepan, add a pinch of salt and bring to the boil. Drop in the dumplings, one by one. Bring back to boiling point then simmer, but do not boil, until the dumplings rise. Turn off the heat and keep covered for another 10 minutes. Then remove from pan and place on a warmed dish. Serve with caster sugar and fresh yoghurt served separately.

Note: This makes a very filling dish and could be used as a main course meal with soup or any starter. The above amounts should make twelve to fifteen dumplings. If frozen, reheat by dropping the dumplings into boiling water and simmering for about 20 minutes until heated through.

Total time: 55 mins.

PINEAPPLE ROLL

	Metric	Imperial	American
Can of pineapple slices	450 g	1 lb	1 lb
Gelatine	1 pkt	1 pkt	1 pkt
Juice of lemon	½	½	½

Drain the juice from the can of pineapple into a small saucepan (leave the pineapple slices in the can). Dissolve the gelatine as directed on packet, using hot fruit juice instead of water. Then make up the required quantity with the remaining fruit juice. Add the lemon juice.

Pour the liquid back into the pineapple can and stand it in a cold place to set. When set, put the tin in warm water almost up to the top for a moment, to loosen the jelly. Carefully turn it out on to a flat serving dish. Place the jelly roll on its side. Cut into slices and serve chilled.

Total time: 10 mins plus setting time.

WITCH'S FLUFF

	Metric	Imperial	American
Egg whites	2	2	2
Caster sugar	1 tbsp	1 tbsp	1 tbsp
Cranberry jelly	3 tbsp	3 tbsp	3 tbsp

Whisk the egg whites until stiff, slowly adding the sugar. Warm the cranberry jelly in a saucepan until it is soft, then fold it into the egg whites. Chill in the refrigerator.

Serve either from a large bowl, or in individual dishes.

Total time: 10 mins.

CAKES

PRUNE LOAF

	Metric	Imperial	American
Prunes, stoned	450 g	1 lb	1 lb
Self-raising flour	150 g	5 oz	1¼ cups
Brown sugar	150 g	5 oz	1¼ cups
Milk	150 ml	¼ pt	⅔ cup

If the stoned prunes are too hard, soak in water, then chop them.

Put all the ingredients into a bowl and mix thoroughly to form a sticky dough. Put into a cake or bread tin and bake in preheated 400°F/200°C/Gas mark 6 oven for 40 minutes.

Remove from oven and immediately loosen by running a knife around the sides. Put a wire tray over the top of the tin, turn it upside down and remove the tin from the loaf. Leave the loaf to cool.

Note: You might find it easier to line the cake tin or bread tin.

Total time: 45 mins.

143

DATE CAKE

	Metric	Imperial	American
Dried dates, sliced and stoned	225 g	8 oz	1/2 lb
Brown sugar	150 g	5 oz	1 cup
Self-raising flour	150 g	5 oz	1¼ cups
Milk	150 ml	¼ pt	⅔ cup

Put all the ingredients into a bowl and mix thoroughly to form a sticky dough. Put into bread or cake tin, place in preheated 400°F/200°C/Gas mark 6 oven and bake for 40 minutes.

When ready, remove from oven and immediately loosen by running a knife round the sides. Remove the cake from the tin and leave to cool.

Note: You might find it easier to line the cake tin.

Total time: 45 mins.

APPLE CAKE

	Metric	Imperial	American
Egg	1	1	1
Egg whites	2	2	2
Caster sugar	175 g	6 oz	¾ cup
Curd or cottage cheese	175 g	6 oz	¾ cup
Self-raising flour	225 g	8 oz	2 cups
Juice and finely grated rind of lemon	½	½	½
Apples, peeled, cored and sliced	3	3	3

Whisk the egg and egg whites together and slowly add the caster sugar. Fold in the cheese and the sifted flour and add the lemon juice and rind. Put the mix into a cake tin.

Insert the thin apple slices upright into the cake mix. Bake in a preheated 325°F/170°C/Gas mark 3 oven for about 1 hour. Before removing from the oven test that the cake is baked through by inserting a knife. The knife should come out clean. When ready, loosen by running a knife around the sides. Remove the cake from the tin, and leave to cool.

This cake is best eaten fresh but it will keep in a cool place if wrapped in kitchen foil. Plums, apricots or cherries can be used instead of apples.

Total time: 1¼ hrs.

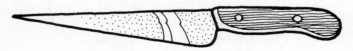

145

CHEESECAKE

	Metric	Imperial	American
Eggs	2	2	2
Egg white	1	1	1
Caster sugar	300 g	10 oz	1¼ cups
Curd or cottage cheese	550 g	1¼ lb	1¼ lb
Baking powder	1 tsp	1 tsp	1 tsp
Semolina	2½ tsp	2½ tsp	2½ tsp
Juice of lemon	1	1	1

Whisk the eggs and the egg white until almost stiff. Add the sugar slowly. Carefully mix in the cheese, the dry ingredients and the lemon juice. Turn into a cake tin, place in preheated 350°F/180°C/Gas mark 4 oven, and bake for about 1¼ hours.

Before taking the cake out of the oven test the centre with a knife. If the blade comes out dry and clean the cake is done. Remove from the oven, allow to cool very slightly, then loosen by running a knife around the sides. Remove the cake from the tin and leave to cool.

Total time: 1½ hrs.

SPONGE KISSES

	Metric	Imperial	American
Egg	1	1	1
Egg white	1	1	1
Caster sugar	50 g	2 oz	¼ cup
Plain flour	50 g	2 oz	½ cup
Jam			

Line the baking tray with baking sheet. Whisk the egg, the egg white and the sugar and fold in the flour. Drop teaspoons of the mix on to the baking tray, keeping them separate. Put into the pre-heated 400°F/200°C/Gas mark 6 oven and bake for 10 minutes.

Remove from the baking sheet, spread each 'kiss' with a little jam, and stick two together.

Note: These 'kisses' can also be decorated with lemon icing and a glacé cherry.

Total time: 30 mins.

HONEY LOAF

	Metric	Imperial	American
Self-raising flour	225 g	8 oz	2 cups
Caster sugar	100 g	4 oz	½ cup
Grated rind of lemon	1	1	1
Honey	2 tbsp	2 tbsp	2 tbsp
Hot water	150 ml	¼ pt	⅔ cup

Mix the flour, sugar and lemon rind in a bowl. Add the honey and hot water and mix well. Turn into a bread tin and bake in a preheated 325°F/170°C/Gas mark 3 oven for one hour.

When cooked, loosen by running a knife round the sides. Remove the cake from the tin and leave to cool. Serve with tea or coffee.

Note: You might find it easier to line the bread tin.

Total time: 1 hr 10 mins.

HONEY CAKE

	Metric	Imperial	American
Self-raising flour	350 g	12 oz	3 cups
Mixed spice	2 tsp	2 tsp	2 tsp
Candied peel	3 tbsp	3 tbsp	3 tbsp
Clear honey	175 g	6 oz	6 oz
Salt	1 pinch	1 pinch	1 pinch
Icing sugar			

Mix all the ingredients, except the icing sugar, in a bowl. Turn into a non-stick baking tin and cook in a preheated 350°F/180°C/Gas mark 4 oven for about one hour.

When cooked, loosen by running a knife round the sides. Remove the cake from the tin and leave to cool. Sprinkle with icing sugar before serving.

Note: You might find it easier to line the baking tin.

Total time: 1 hr 10 mins.

SPONGE CAKE

	Metric	Imperial	American
Egg	1	1	1
Egg whites	2	2	2
Caster sugar	85 g	3 oz	¾ cup
Self-raising flour	85 g	3 oz	¾ cup
Jam	4 tbsp	4 tbsp	4 tbsp
Icing sugar	25 g	1 oz	2 tbsp

Preheat the oven to 325°F/170°C/Gas mark 3. Whisk egg and egg whites vigorously, gradually adding caster sugar. Sieve the flour and fold half into the mixture with a metal spoon. Then fold in the remainder, but do not overmix. Put into a cake tin. Place in the preheated oven and bake for 45 minutes. Remove from oven, take the cake out of the tin and leave to cool. When cold, slice in half, spread bottom with jam, cover with the top and sprinkle with icing sugar.

Total time: 1 hr.

SWISS ROLL

	Metric	Imperial	American
Eggs	2	2	2
Egg white	1	1	1
Caster sugar	100 g	4 oz	½ cup
Self-raising flour	100 g	4 oz	1 cup
Icing sugar			
Warmed jam	3 tbsp	3 tbsp	3 tbsp

Break the eggs into a bowl and whisk, slowly adding the caster sugar, until the mix is stiff. Slowly fold in the sifted flour with a metal spoon. Line a baking tin with greaseproof paper and cover it thinly with the mixture.

Bake in the preheated 350°F/180°C/Gas mark 4 oven for about 10 minutes.

Lightly dust a piece of greaseproof paper with icing sugar and turn the roll out on to it. Spread with warmed jam. To form the roll, take the edge of the greaseproof paper nearest to you and gently lift away from you with a rolling movement. When the roll is cool, sprinkle with a little icing sugar.

Total time: 30 mins.

FAKE HAZELNUT CAKE

	Metric	Imperial	American
Egg whites	4	4	4
Egg yolks	2	2	2
Juice and grated rind of lemon	1	1	1
Caster sugar	100 g	4 oz	½ cup
Vanilla sugar	50 g	2 oz	¼ cup
OR			
Vanilla essence	½ tbsp	½ tbsp	½ tbsp
Bread crumbs from brown bread	150 g	6 oz	¾ cup

Mix the egg yolks with the caster sugar. Add the lemon juice, rind and bread crumbs. Whisk the egg whites with vanilla sugar or essence until quite stiff. Carefully fold the two mixes together. Turn into a baking tin and bake in a preheated 300°F/150°C/Gas mark 2 oven for 1 hour.

When cooked, loosen by running a knife round the sides. Remove the cake from the tin and leave to cool. When cold, slice in half, spread the bottom half with blackcurrant or redcurrant jelly, and put the top back.

Total time: 1 hour 10 mins.

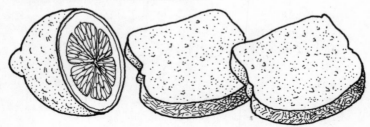

151

FILLED SPONGE CAKE

	Metric	Imperial	American
Sponge cake (Page 149)	1	1	1
Curd cheese	225 g	8 oz	½ lb
Caster sugar	2 tbsp	2 tbsp	2 tbsp
Apricot jam	2 tbsp	2 tbsp	2 tbsp

Make the sponge cake. Whisk the cheese and sugar. When the cake is cold, slice it in half and spread both halves with apricot jam. Spread the bottom part with the cheese and cover with the top. Serve as a dessert or with tea or coffee.

Note: This cake can also be used uncut and covered with fresh strawberries or raspberries sprinkled with sugar.

Total time: 1 hr.

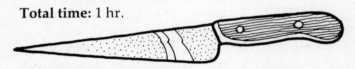

FRUIT CAKE

	Metric	Imperial	American
Sultanas	700 g	1½ lb	4 cups
Tea (minimum)	300 ml	½ pt	1¼ cups
Juice of lemon	½	½	½
Self-raising flour	700 g	1½ lb	6 cups
Demerara sugar	350 g	12 oz	2 cups
Eggs	2	2	2
Egg white	1	1	1

The evening before you bake the cake, put the sultanas into a pudding basin and cover with tea. When the tea is soaked up, add more tea so that the sultanas are saturated. Leave to soak overnight.

Next day, put the flour into a mixing bowl and add the sugar, eggs, egg white and lemon juice and the sultana–tea mixture. Mix thoroughly. The dough is at the right consistency when it becomes sticky.

Divide the dough equally between two cake or baking tins and bake in a preheated 325°F/170°C/ Gas mark 3 oven for 1½ hours.

Before taking out the cakes, test with a knife. If the blade comes out dry and clean, the cake is done. Take the cakes out of the oven and immediately loosen by running a knife round the sides. Remove the cakes from the tins and leave to cool.

Note: It is possible to use only the whites of three eggs, and no yolks, if you prefer. You may find it easier to remove the cakes if you line the baking tins. This cake will keep for a long time if wrapped in kitchen foil or cling film so the quantities given are for two cakes. You will find that they will be eaten very quickly.

Total time: 1 hr 35 mins plus overnight soaking.

MADEIRA TYPE CAKE

	Metric	Imperial	American
Self-raising flour	225 g	8 oz	2 cups
Caster sugar	150 g	6 oz	¾ cup
Whole eggs	2	2	2
Egg white	1	1	1
Curd cheese	150 g	6 oz	⅓ lb
Grated rind of lemon	1	1	1
Lemon juice	2 tbsp	2 tbsp	2 tbsp

Mix the caster sugar and curd cheese. Add the lemon juice, lemon rind and eggs. Mix well. Sieve the flour, and fold half into the mixture with a metal spoon. Then fold in the remainder. Do not overmix. Line the baking tin and bake in pre-heated 325°F/170°C/Gas mark 3 oven for 50 minutes.

When cooked, remove the cake from the tin and leave to cool.

Total time: 1 hr.

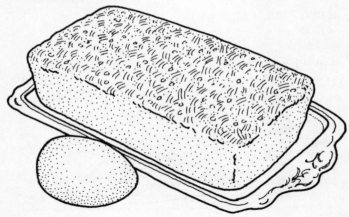

POMMES BRISTOL

	Metric	Imperial	American
Large eating apples cored, peeled and sliced	4	4	4
Water	300 ml	½ pt	1 ⅓ cup
Sugar	3 tbsp	3 tbsp	3 tbsp
Vanilla essence	½ tbsp	½ tbsp	½ tbsp
Oranges	3	3	3

Put the water into a saucepan, add the sugar and vanilla essence and dissolve the sugar over gentle heat. Add the sliced apples and simmer for about 10 minutes until they are transparent. Allow to cool. Remove the outer skin of the oranges with a sharp knife, leaving the pith on. Cut into thin slices and simmer separately for 5 minutes. Drain and rinse in cold water. Remove the pith from the oranges and slice thinly. Put the cooled apples and juice into a dish, add the orange peel and decorate with the sliced oranges. Serve chilled.

Total time: 25 mins.

BREAD

CRUSTY LOAF

	Metric	Imperial	American
Wholewheat flour	225 g	8 oz	½ lb
Self-raising flour	125 g	4 oz	1 cup
Brown sugar	2 tsp	2 tsp	2 tsp
Salt	2 tsp	2 tsp	2 tsp
Bicarbonate of soda	1 tsp	1 tsp	1 tsp
Water	150 ml	¼ pt	⅔ cup
Milk	150 ml	¼ pt	⅔ cup

Put all the dry ingredients into a bowl and mix thoroughly. Make a well in the middle, add the liquid and mix into a dough. Line the bread tin with a baking sheet and transfer the dough into it. Score the top with a knife, once lengthways and twice across. Bake in a preheated 400°F/200°C/Gas mark 6 oven for 50 minutes.

Total time: 1 hr.

WHITE BREAD

	Metric	Imperial	American
White flour, sieved	450 g	1 lb	4 cups
Fresh yeast	12 g	½ oz	1 tbsp
Salt	½ tbsp	½ tbsp	½ tbsp
Milk and water mixed and warmed	250 ml	½ pt	1 ⅓ cup
Sugar	½ tbsp	½ tbsp	½ tbsp

Put the flour and salt into a mixing bowl. Mix the yeast with a little sugar until liquid. Make a well in the centre of the flour, pour in the yeast and all the liquid. Mix with a wooden spoon until it clears. Turn onto a floured board and knead for about 10 minutes until the dough is smooth. Place the dough into a greased polythene bag, and leave to rise until it is double its size. Turn risen dough back onto a floured board and knead, to force out all air bubbles.

Line two ½ lb bread tins, and turn the dough into them. Cover with a sheet of polythene and leave until they rise to the top of the tin. Bake in a preheated 400°F/200°C/Gas mark 6 oven for 10 minutes, then lower the setting to 375°F/190°C/Gas mark 5 for about 30 minutes. When cooked, remove loaves to cool.

Total time: 1½ hrs.

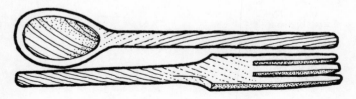

INDEX

160